Credits

Author
Scott Faranello

Reviewers
Paul Daly
Anthony J. Moffa
Rob Mousley

Acquisition Editor
Wilson D'Souza

Lead Technical Editor
Kedar Bhat

Technical Editors
Dipesh Panchal
Devdutt Kulkarni

Copy Editor
Laxmi Subramanian

Project Coordinator
Michelle Quadros

Proofreader
Linda Morris

Indexer
Hemangini Bari

Production Coordinator
Prachali Bhiwandkar

Cover Work
Prachali Bhiwandkar

About the Author

Scott Faranello's work in the field of user experience design and architecture has led him on an impressive journey. From Graphic Designer and Consultant to award-winning User Experience Designer, Director of UX, and now Customer Experience Architect and Marketing Product Manager, Scott has created an extensive list of credentials having worked for some of the largest companies in the U.S. and the world. His extensive portfolio includes working with GM (U.S. and Europe), GE, Ford Motors, United Airlines, and most recently with one of the world's largest healthcare organizations where he is helping to shape the future of customer experience within the industry. Scott's work has been seen and used by literally millions of end users around the world and in a multitude of industries including corporate, security, finance, entertainment, travel, telecommunication, software development, B2B, e-commerce, and healthcare. A native New Yorker, Scott currently resides in Connecticut and holds a Bachelor's degree in Human Computer Interaction and History from DePaul University, Chicago, IL.

> I would like to thank, first and foremost, my beautiful wife and two boys. You inspire me to be my best. I would also like to thank the great folks at Packt Publishing for making my first book such a fun and professional experience. Your dedication and care towards quality makes me proud to be a part of the team. Last, but not least, thanks to the folks who took the time to review my work and helped me to make it the best book possible. I am grateful.

Balsamiq Wireframes Quickstart Guide

Wireframe like a pro, the easy way

Scott Faranello

[PACKT]
PUBLISHING

BIRMINGHAM - MUMBAI

Balsamiq Wireframes Quickstart Guide

Copyright © 2012 Packt Publishing

All rights reserved. No part of this book may be reproduced, stored in a retrieval system, or transmitted in any form or by any means, without the prior written permission of the publisher, except in the case of brief quotations embedded in critical articles or reviews.

Every effort has been made in the preparation of this book to ensure the accuracy of the information presented. However, the information contained in this book is sold without warranty, either express or implied. Neither the author, nor Packt Publishing, and its dealers and distributors will be held liable for any damages caused or alleged to be caused directly or indirectly by this book.

Packt Publishing has endeavored to provide trademark information about all of the companies and products mentioned in this book by the appropriate use of capitals. However, Packt Publishing cannot guarantee the accuracy of this information.

First published: September 2012

Production Reference: 1180912

Published by Packt Publishing Ltd.
Livery Place
35 Livery Street
Birmingham B3 2PB, UK.

ISBN 978-1-84969-352-3

www.packtpub.com

Cover Image by Artie Ng (artherng@yahoo.com.au)

About the Reviewers

Paul Daly is a User Experience Designer who has worked with companies including USAA, Texas Instruments, and Emerson Process Management on the usability of services/work processes, multi-platform desktop software and systems, websites, and mobile devices. He uses whatever he can get his hands on to mockup or prototype — paper, HyperCard, Authorware, HTML, Photoshop, PowerPoint, Axure, Expression Blend, and now Balsamiq—whatever it takes to get the point across and get feedback from users.

Anthony Moffa is an Information Architect and User Experience Analyst. He has practiced professionally for over 15 years for clients such as Oracle, SAP, and most recently the Patient Marketing Group of inVentiv Co. Anthony enjoys creating wireframes and prototypes for user interfaces, and routinely searches for new tools for producing these artifacts. Several years ago, he discovered Balsamiq Mockups and has used it regularly ever since. Anthony also likes to write and edit, and is thrilled to have reviewed this book about Balsamiq Mockups. Anthony holds an M.S. degree in Engineering Psychology from the Florida Institute of Technology.

Rob Mousley has a passion for creating software solutions. He's been doing it on and off for nearly 25 years and still gets a buzz from user feedback. He believes that the essence of user experience design is making users love the software.

www.PacktPub.com

Support files, eBooks, discount offers and more

You might want to visit www.PacktPub.com for support files and downloads related to your book.

Did you know that Packt offers eBook versions of every book published, with PDF and ePub files available? You can upgrade to the eBook version at www.PacktPub.com and as a print book customer, you are entitled to a discount on the eBook copy. Get in touch with us at service@packtpub.com for more details.

At www.PacktPub.com, you can also read a collection of free technical articles, sign up for a range of free newsletters and receive exclusive discounts and offers on Packt books and eBooks.

PACKTLIB

http://PacktLib.PacktPub.com

Do you need instant solutions to your IT questions? PacktLib is Packt's online digital book library. Here, you can access, read, and search across Packt's entire library of books.

Why Subscribe?

- Fully searchable across every book published by Packt
- Copy and paste, print and bookmark content
- On demand and accessible via web browser

Free Access for Packt account holders

If you have an account with Packt at www.PacktPub.com, you can use this to access PacktLib today and view nine entirely free books. Simply use your login credentials for immediate access.

Table of Contents

Preface	**1**
Chapter 1: Getting to Know Balsamiq	**7**
What is Balsamiq?	**8**
Installing Balsamiq	**8**
System requirements	8
Installation	9
What is Adobe Air?	9
Balsamiq Mockups versus myBalsamiq	10
Trial versus paid version	10
The application	**10**
Application menu	10
New Clone of Current Mockup	11
Save All	11
Close All	11
Export to PNG Image	12
Export All Mockups to PNG	13
Export All Mockups to PDF	13
Export Image to Clipboard	13
Export Mockup XML	13
Import Mockup XML	14
Application view	14
Application Bar	15
UI Library	17
Canvas	18
File Browser	18
Property Inspector	20
Summary	**20**

Table of Contents

Chapter 2: Building a Project — 21
The project files — 21
Organizing your Balsamiq files — 22
Naming your files — 22
Alphabetically — 22
Numbering — 22
The project — 23
So what are we building? — 23
The UI Library revisited — 24
Adding a widget — 24
Alignment — 25
Layering — 26
Grouping layers — 28
Putting it all together — 29
Before we begin: A brief word about design and layout — 29
Rectangle/Canvas/Panel — 30
Adding text — 31
Images — 32
Align tool — 33
The body copy — 34
Summary — 35

Chapter 3: Working with Symbols — 37
What are symbols? — 37
Creating a symbol — 38
Location of the saved symbols — 39
Symbols.bmml — 40
Symbols as a master page — 40
Modifying a symbol — 40
Page by page — 40
All pages — 41
Additional ways to edit a symbol — 42
Break Apart — 42
Edit Source — 42
Project Assets — 42
Reverting to saved — 42
Deleting a symbol — 43
Page by page — 43
All pages — 43
Revisiting the wireframe project — 44
Adding symbols to multiple pages — 44
Copying and pasting the symbol — 45
Dragging the symbol — 46
Double-clicking on the symbol — 46

Creating a new symbol	46
Adding some text	46
Adding the footer to all pages	47
Creating a symbol library	**47**
Adding the symbol to your project	48
Sharing symbols	**50**
Project by project	50
All projects	50
Summary	**51**
Chapter 4: Building Data Tables	**53**
Data tables	**53**
Formatting data	**55**
Deciphering the data	**55**
Columns and rows: A closer look	56
Grid form elements	56
Width and alignment controls	57
Data table tips	**59**
Highlighting a table row	59
Adding a scroll bar	60
Wireframe project revisited	**60**
Revising your project	61
Action Bar	61
Data table	63
Paging	65
Even more tips	**67**
Formatting: Readability is usability	67
Data table details	67
Learn more/see more	67
Padding table columns	68
Aligning text	68
Maximum column width	68
Mac and PC compatibility issues	68
Summary	**69**
Chapter 5: Icons, Images, and Text	**71**
Exploring icons	**71**
Importing icons	**73**
The Icon Library	74
Images	**77**
The Load Image window	78
Copying images to project assets	79
Image not found	80
Cropping images	80

Table of Contents

Text usage and formatting	**82**
Additional text tools	83
Combining formatting styles	84
Single line text versus paragraph	84
Additional tips	**86**
Lorem ipsum	87
Sketch it!	87
Auto-Size	88
Summary	**88**
Chapter 6: Presenting Your Work	**89**
Prototyping	**89**
Symbols revisited	90
Linking pages	**91**
Presentation mode	92
Link types	92
The other two icons	94
Additional interactivity	**94**
Interactive checkbox	95
Even more interactivity	97
Notes and documentation (also known as markup)	**100**
Markup widgets	101
Exporting for Presentation	**102**
Exporting to PDF	102
Exporting to PNG	104
Exporting a single page to PNG	104
Exporting individual elements to PNG	104
Exporting an entire project to PNG	105
Exporting an image to the clipboard	105
XML in Balsamiq	**106**
Exporting wireframes as XML	106
Importing XML	107
Summary	**109**
Chapter 7: Parting Thoughts: Resources and Recommendations	**111**
More about Balsamiq	**112**
Balsamiq blog	112
Balsamiq support	113
Record a Screencast	113
Ask the community	115
Keyboard shortcuts	117

[iv]

Table of Contents

Third-party extensions	**117**
Napkee	117
MockupsToGo	117
Reality Mechanic	118
LiveMockups	118
Wirify by Volkside	118
Project management	119
Further reading	**119**
Books	119
Usability websites	120
One final tip	121
Summary	**122**
Index	**123**

Preface

I was first introduced to Balsamiq while working as the Director of User Experience for a software company in Chicago. Until that point in my career, I had been designing user interfaces and clickable prototypes using Photoshop, handcoding layouts in HTML and CSS, and spending a lot of time learning prototype software like iRise and Axure.

Now, these are all great tools and should be explored fully. But, my role with this company was different. I was working as a user-experience architect alongside a large agile team of developers. In an environment such as this, it meant that I no longer had the luxury of time to transform my ideas into hi-fidelity layouts and complex clickable prototypes. Instead, I now had to work faster, more efficiently, and deliver creative concepts that were clear and concise, but in a fraction of time. There was simply no time to wireframe in Photoshop or code HTML, and to be honest, Axure was just too cumbersome, personally speaking, for doing quick and dirty designs that my development team demanded. Then, I discovered Balsamiq.

I was first introduced to Balsamiq by a developer on my team. He had been using it to sketch rough ideas to share with his development colleagues. Of course, I was immediately impressed. After all, developers are not known as the visual folks on the team, as much as working with detailed, text heavy requirements, and raw programming code. So, when I learned that a developer was already using the tool effectively, I knew I had to learn more.

From the moment I launched Balsamiq Mockups, its value was immediately apparent. Gone were the complicated toolbars with multiple menu options to learn. Gone too were the long hours toiling over hi-fidelity Photoshop mockups or tweaking handcoded HTML and CSS. With Balsamiq, I was able to design simple, concise, and effective designs using simple graphics and in half the time! As a result, my development team could immediately see what I wanted and could ask the right questions early. Plus, with Balsamiq's ability to make simple, clickable prototypes, I could impressively present my ideas to the team with ease.

Preface

With Balsamiq, I found a tool that let me express my ideas without the pressure of having to be perfect. I was also able to design with the same creative intention, but on a very basic and raw level. The focus became less about the tool I was using and more about the architecture of the design. In other words, with Balsamiq, I had found the tool I had always been looking for. I am sure you will agree.

What this book covers

Chapter 1, Getting to Know Balsamiq, starts with the basics of Balsamiq and walks you through the installation and the ins-and-outs of the application. Learn important menu items and about the application screen itself, setting the stage or what's to come.

Chapter 2, Building a Project, is a continuation of the essential elements of Balsamiq - like layering, alignment, and grouping, as well as an introduction to the project work you will be completing throughout the remainder of the book.

Chapter 3, Working with Symbols, discusses one of the more useful tools in Balsamiq. Symbols allow you to work more productively by allowing you to take greater control over your wireframes.

Chapter 4, Building Data Tables, deals with deciphering and presenting data online, one of the key challenges of great user interface design. Often, it could mean taking Excel data and making it interesting for your site's visitors. Not an easy thing to do. This chapter will walk you through good data table design and explain how to present data that is readable, useable, and presented effectively with Balsamiq.

Chapter 5, Icons, Images, and Text, presents you with three elements that are vital to a successful user experience. Knowing how to use each of them could make or break your entire design. In this chapter, we walk through these essential elements and demonstrate how to use them effectively in Balsamiq.

Chapter 6, Presenting Your Work, teaches you how to present your work to an outside audience. Whether you are creating a clickable prototype, a printable PDF, or exporting your work as a raw XML code, Balsamiq does it all with ease. This chapter shows you how.

Chapter 7, Parting Thoughts: Resources and Recommendations, will leave you with some very useful books, websites, and general tips that take what you have learned using this book and Balsamiq to the next level in terms of skill, creativity, and career.

What you need for this book

This book is complete with multiple real-world examples using Balsamiq. As a result, you will need a few things to get the most out of your learning experience:

- A copy of Balsamiq, which you can download at: http://www.balsamiq.com/download. While the initial download is free, it will expire after seven days.
- All of the examples in this book, including screenshots, were created using a MacBook Pro. However, these should all work similarly on a PC.
- A connection to the Internet is recommended, as the files for the exercises are downloadable.

Who this book is for

This book is for anyone serious about wireframing, designing, prototyping, and communicating user interface design ideas.

That means:

- User Experience (UX) professionals
- Developers looking to visualize their ideas to colleagues
- Product Managers
- Graphic Designers
- Anyone else who wants to convey ideas quickly and easily

Conventions

In this book, you will find a number of styles of text that distinguish between different kinds of information. Here are some examples of these styles, and an explanation of their meaning.

Code words in text are shown as follows: "Click the arrows until the **Pos** numbers read: `79,260`".

Preface

New terms and **important words** are shown in bold. Words that you see on the screen, in menus or dialog boxes for example, appear in the text like this: "Locate the widget called **Video Player** from the UI Library."

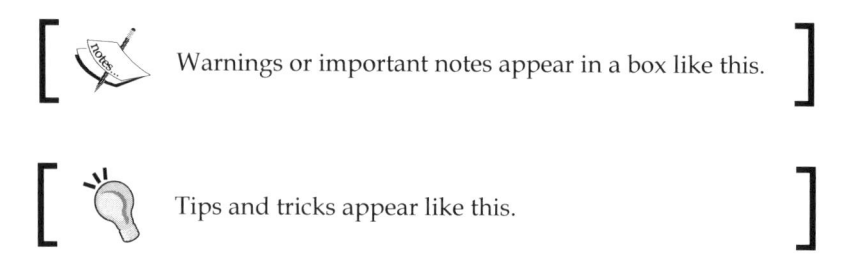

> Warnings or important notes appear in a box like this.

> Tips and tricks appear like this.

Reader feedback

Feedback from our readers is always welcome. Let us know what you think about this book—what you liked or may have disliked. Reader feedback is important for us to develop titles that you really get the most out of.

To send us general feedback, simply send an e-mail to feedback@packtpub.com, and mention the book title through the subject of your message.

If there is a topic that you have expertise in and you are interested in either writing or contributing to a book, see our author guide on www.packtpub.com/authors.

Customer support

Now that you are the proud owner of a Packt book, we have a number of things to help you to get the most from your purchase.

Downloading the example code

You can download the example code files for all Packt books you have purchased from your account at http://www.packtpub.com. If you purchased this book elsewhere, you can visit http://www.packtpub.com/support and register to have the files e-mailed directly to you.

Errata

Although we have taken every care to ensure the accuracy of our content, mistakes do happen. If you find a mistake in one of our books—maybe a mistake in the text or the code—we would be grateful if you would report this to us. By doing so, you can save other readers from frustration and help us improve subsequent versions of this book. If you find any errata, please report them by visiting http://www.packtpub.com/support, selecting your book, clicking on the **errata submission form** link, and entering the details of your errata. Once your errata are verified, your submission will be accepted and the errata will be uploaded to our website, or added to any list of existing errata, under the Errata section of that title.

Piracy

Piracy of copyright material on the Internet is an ongoing problem across all media. At Packt, we take the protection of our copyright and licenses very seriously. If you come across any illegal copies of our works, in any form, on the Internet, please provide us with the location address or website name immediately so that we can pursue a remedy.

Please contact us at copyright@packtpub.com with a link to the suspected pirated material.

We appreciate your help in protecting our authors, and our ability to bring you valuable content.

Questions

You can contact us at questions@packtpub.com if you are having a problem with any aspect of the book, and we will do our best to address it.

Getting to Know Balsamiq

Welcome to Balsamiq Prototyping. It is a pleasure having you along for this practical exploration of Balsamiq Mockups. During the course of this book, we are going to explore everything there is to know about this wonderfully simple, yet powerful application; from understanding the application's interface, building a functional and professional wireframe, and finishing with a basic, clickable prototype to show off as part of your professional wireframe portfolio.

In fact, by the time you finish with this book, you will have become an expert in using Balsamiq and you will be able to express your ideas to their fullest and most professionally.

We will begin with the basics of the application and then move on to building a real-world wireframe project. As you progress through each chapter, you will also build upon what you have learned in the previous chapters. Finally, we will review and leave you with tips and resources to take your newly acquired skills to the next level.

In this chapter, we will cover the following:

- What is Balsamiq?
- Installing Balsamiq
- The application

Let's dive right in!

What is Balsamiq?

To understand Balsamiq is to understand wireframing. Wireframing is, of course, the sketching out of ideas for a product or web interface in skeletal form, depicting at a high level what it will do, how it might look, and how it will function. Prior to Balsamiq and other similar applications, wireframing was traditionally done by hand on paper, or by using applications like Visio and/or Photoshop.

While these are fine in their own right, Balsamiq offers things others do not. They are as follows:

- Ease of use: You will be creating wireframes moments after you open the application.
- Simple Tools: Balsamiq is filled with easy-to-understand visual tools that will help you to transfer your ideas from your head to the screen quickly and clearly.
- Portability: Balsamiq files can be easily shared among your peers and clients alike. With Balsamiq, you will be designing and sharing your work across multiple operating systems and with whomever you choose via e-mail, in print, or online.
- Affordability: Balsamiq is at a price everyone can appreciate. And that is because Balsamiq really does just one thing: wireframing. But, as you will soon see, it does that very, very well.

But enough talk! To really understand, experience, and enjoy Balsamiq, you have to use it. So let's get started.

Installing Balsamiq

While installing Balsamiq is pretty straightforward, what instructional book would be complete without showing you how?

System requirements

Balsamiq will run on Windows, Mac, and Linux. You will also need to download an application called Adobe Air, but more on that later.

> The examples in this book were created using the Macintosh operating system. Nevertheless, the instructions and examples that follow will work on whatever platform you choose to run the application.

Installation

Please note that these instructions are for the Macintosh operating system. However, installing on a PC should be a similar experience. Perform the following steps to install Balsamiq:

1. Open a browser and type in `http://www.balsamiq.com/download`.
2. Once at the Balsamiq website, click on the **Install Mockups** button to begin installation, as shown in the following screenshot:

   You can also download the installation files by scrolling down the page and clicking on the link **Mac OSX: MockupsForDesktop.dmg** and similarly for other operating systems as well.

3. Once the installation has started, you may see a pop-up message telling you that an application called Adobe Air will be downloaded to your computer. Click on **Yes** to continue with the installation, as shown in the following screenshot:

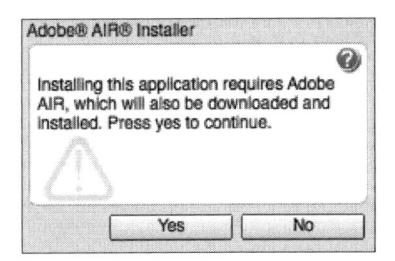

4. Read and accept the Adobe license agreement to complete the installation. Once installed, Balsamiq should open automatically on your desktop.

What is Adobe Air?

Adobe Air is a cross-platform development environment that allows web developers to create rich web applications and content that is downloadable directly from the Web. As you will see, Balsamiq is essentially a drag-and-drop application with Flash-like capabilities. The Adobe Air application that installs on your machine makes that functionality possible.

Getting to Know Balsamiq

Balsamiq Mockups versus myBalsamiq

When you go to the Balsamiq website to download the application, you will see two application types. One is Balsamiq Mockups and the other is myBalsamiq. The difference between these two is simple. The first is downloadable directly to your computer. The other is a pay-for-use cloud-based application that you access via your web browser.

> While I have not tested myBalsamiq, I assume it works exactly like Balsamiq Mockups for the desktop. The major difference would be that MyBalsamiq is cloud-based and requires an Internet connection, while Mockups does not. Regardless, this book assumes and presents material as if you have downloaded Balsamiq Mockups directly to your computer's hard drive.

Trial versus paid version

When you install Balsamiq onto your computer, it will open automatically to a blank canvas. You will then have access to the entire application for free. However, keep in mind that, at this point, Balsamiq is only a trial version and will expire after seven days.

To purchase Balsamiq at any time during your trial, simply return to the Balsamiq website and click on **BUY** located at the top navigation bar. At the time of publishing this book, a single user license costs $79. It is worth every penny.

The application

With Balsamiq now installed and opened on your computer's desktop, you are essentially looking at the entirety of the application. Let's break it down into its essential pieces. There are two main areas of focus:

1. Application menu
2. Application view

Application menu

The Application menu, like any menu found in most applications, is found at the top of your computer screen, as shown in the following screenshot:

While most of the items found within these menus are common to all applications, like Save, Open, New, Cut, Copy, Paste, and so on, there are a few that are specific to Balsamiq and that may be helpful to you when working with the tool.

The ones I am referring to can be found under the **File** menu, as shown in the following screenshot:

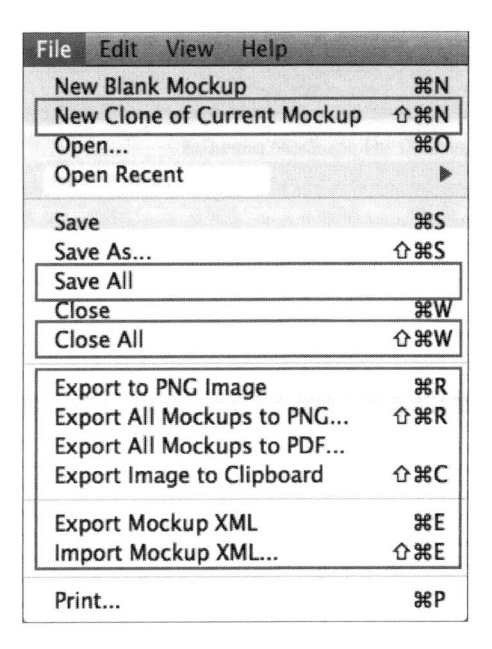

New Clone of Current Mockup

This menu item acts as it sounds by making a duplicate of whatever Balsamiq page is currently active on your screen.

Save All

This command will save any changes made to multiple pages currently open on your screen. As you will most definitely be working with multiple pages, I am sure you will find this tool to be very useful.

Close All

This command will close all open pages in the application at once.

Getting to Know Balsamiq

Export to PNG Image

Selecting this command from the **File** menu saves the entire active page as a `.png` file. You can also use this command to save parts of a page by performing the following steps:

1. Press the *Shift* key on your computer keyboard as you select individual elements on the canvas.
2. Select **Export to PNG Image** from the **File** menu.

If you choose to save only a portion of the screen, you will see a dialog box with the option to save only what you selected (**Export Selected**). Or, if you so choose, you can save the entire page with one click (**Export Everything**), as shown in the following screenshot:

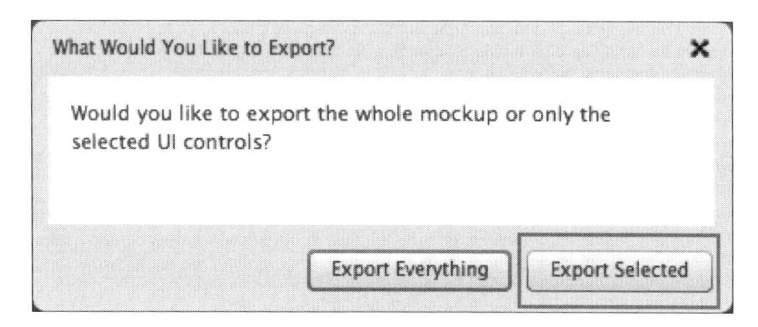

Upon exporting your work, a dialog box will appear telling you where exactly the `.png` file was saved, as shown in the following screenshot:

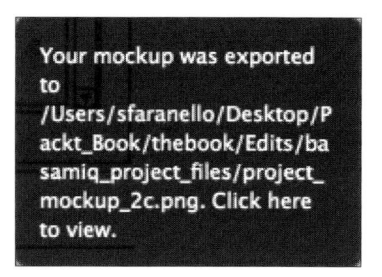

Balsamiq mockup files use the file extension `.bmml`, which stands for **Balsamiq Mockups Markup Language**.

> For the sake of consistency, and for the remainder of this book, we will refer to all mockup files as .bmml files.

[12]

Export All Mockups to PNG

Unlike the previous command which saved only the active page as a single `.png` file, this command will save every open page as a separate `.png` file.

Export All Mockups to PDF

Choosing this command converts all of your open `.bmml` files into a single, multi-page PDF document that you can print, email, use for building paper prototypes, share with peers, or present to a larger group.

Export Image to Clipboard

This menu item copies the contents of an entire canvas, or some selected elements of the canvas, onto the clipboard. Once that is done, the content can then be pasted onto a new Balsamiq canvas or into any application that accepts images like Photoshop, MS Word, PowerPoint, and so on.

> When copying items to the clipboard in Balsamiq, you must use **Export Image to Clipboard**. If you try to copy to the clipboard using just *Command + C* or *Ctrl + C*, Balsamiq will transform the contents into raw XML code. Give it a try to see for yourself.

Export Mockup XML

Speaking of raw XML code, **Export Mockup XML** will export an entire `.bmml` file into raw XML code. From there, the XML code can be imported into another Balsamiq page or saved as pure XML code to share with other developers. When selecting this command, you will see the following pop-up message confirming the action:

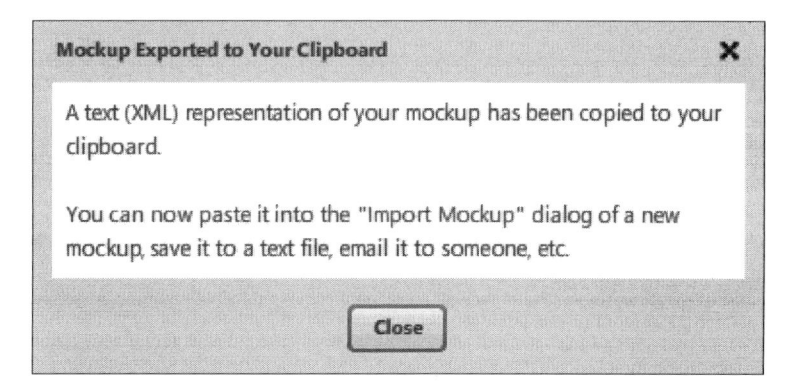

Mockup Exported to Your Clipboard

A text (XML) representation of your mockup has been copied to your clipboard.

You can now paste it into the "Import Mockup" dialog of a new mockup, save it to a text file, email it to someone, etc.

Close

Getting to Know Balsamiq

Import Mockup XML

To import XML code back into a `.bmml` file, open a new canvas (*Command + N* or *Ctrl + N*) and paste your copied XML code into the text field that appears, as shown in the following screenshot:

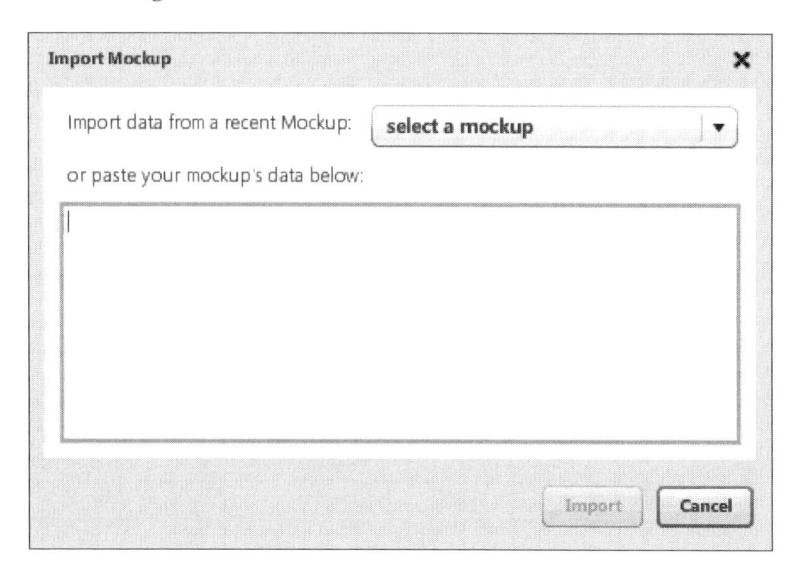

If you want to import an entire page as XML, click the menu item called **select a mockup** and select a page from the drop-down menu. Once a selection is made, the **Import** button will become active.

> Importing XML code into a mockup will over write whatever was on the page. Use this command only when importing XML code into a new, blank canvas page.

Application view

Now let's take a closer look at Balsamiq's main application window. This is where you will be spending most of your time.

The application window in the following screenshot, shown here in full, can be broken down into four distinct areas:

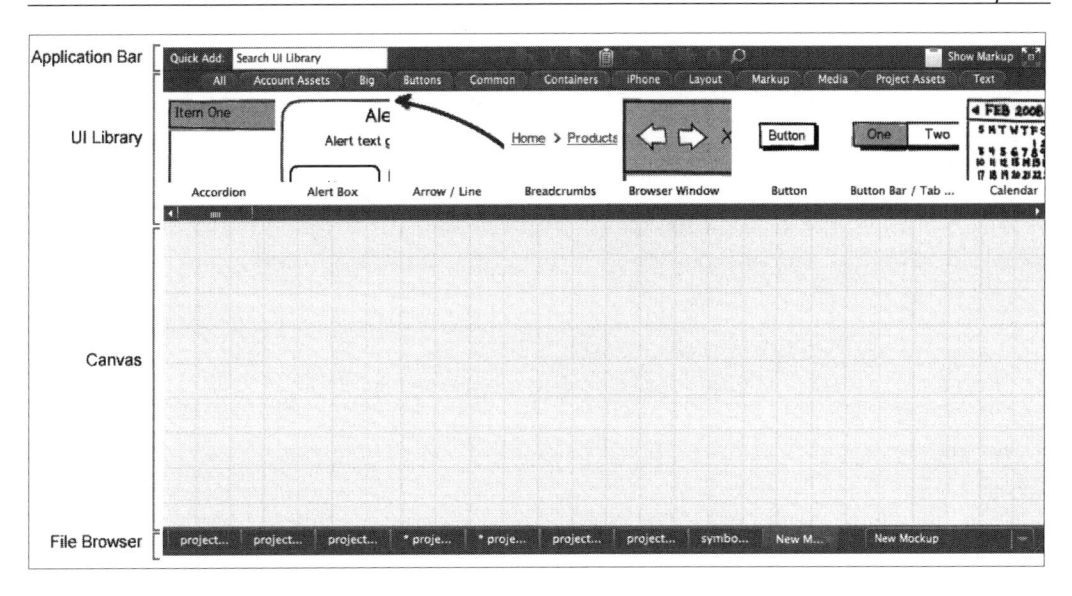

Application Bar

The Application Bar sits atop the main application window and contains some of the most commonly used Balsamiq tools.

Quick Add

Starting in the upper-left of the application bar, you will find the **Quick Add** tool, as shown in the following screenshot:

This tool allows you to find items in the UI Library quickly by typing a letter or word into the text field, utilizing a Google-like autocomplete functionality, as shown in the following screenshot:

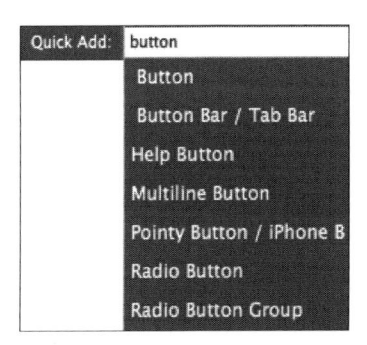

Select the most appropriate result in the results list and press **Enter** on your keyboard. The chosen widget will appear on the canvas. Give it a try.

Tool Bar

The Tool Bar offers many of the same tools found in the **Edit** menu at the top of the screen. However, rather than having to go up to the **Edit** menu for items like Undo, Redo, Duplicate, Cut, Copy, Paste, and so on, the **Tool Bar** gives them to you in a more convenient, one-click location, as shown in the following screenshot:

To learn the name of an icon within the Property Inspector, simply hover your mouse pointer over an icon and wait until you see its name in the tooltip provided.

Show Markup

Balsamiq allows you to add notes to your wireframe to note things like user instructions, special notes to the developers, explanations of complicated areas, numbering of items, and so on. These notes are referred to in Balsamiq as markup. By clicking on the **Show Markup** button, you can toggle markup on and off, as shown in the following screenshot:

Creating markup in Balsamiq is easy. Just click the button labeled **Markup** in the UI Library to filter just those widgets, as shown in the following screenshot:

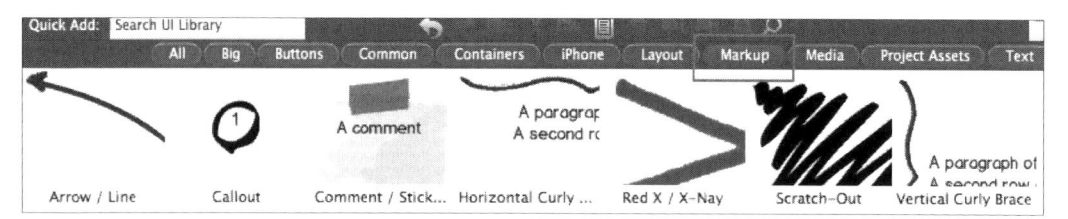

We will be taking a closer look at markup in *Chapter 6, Presenting Your Work*.

Full Screen (Presentation Mode)

Full Screen (Presentation Mode) is a one-click toggle button that resizes Balsamiq to full screen. You will use this functionality when you start presenting your work to clients, or if you want to demonstrate some interactivity using a clickable prototype.

We will learn more about Balsamiq's prototyping capabilities, in *Chapter 6, Presenting your Work*.

To return to the smaller screen, simply click the *Esc* key on your computer keyboard.

UI Library

The UI Library is the part of the Balsamiq application that you will be using often as you build your wireframes. Each graphical element within the library is referred to as a widget. Simply click-and-drag, or double-click on a widget, and it will appear on your canvas, as shown in the following screenshot:

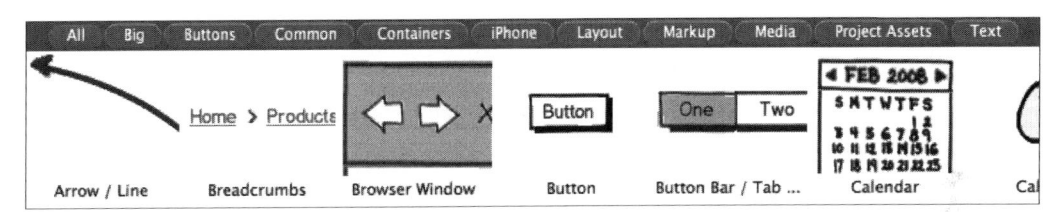

As you can see in the previous screenshot, there are quite a few widgets to choose from. Rather than defining each one here, they are introduced throughout the remainder of this book.

> To view a complete description for every widget in the UI Library, visit `https://support.mybalsamiq.com/projects/uilibrary/story`.

To use the UI Library, click a button just above the UI Library to isolate a specific category of widgets, or simply click on the **All** button, scroll to the desired element, and drag it onto the canvas. You can also double-click on a widget to place it on the canvas.

> While the location of the UI Library bar defaults to the top of the application window, you have the option to move it to the left or to the right by choosing the **View** menu at the top of the screen and selecting **Library Position | Top, Left, Right** from the drop-down menu.

Getting to Know Balsamiq

Canvas

The canvas acts as a blank sheet of paper upon which you build your ideas and turn them into working wireframes. Just place some widgets from the UI Library onto your canvas and start building. For more on working with the canvas, explore *Chapter 2, Building a Project*.

File Browser

At the very bottom of the application window is the File Browser. Each open canvas page is shown as a tab containing the name of that file. Since you can only work on one page at a time in Balsamiq, the currently active page is highlighted in blue, as shown in the following screenshot:

There are a few things to note about the file browser:

- Viewing pages: Click on the tab of the page you want to work on.
- Rearranging pages: While clicking on a page tab, drag it left or right and to its new position in the File Browser.
- Closing a page: Click on the x icon located to the right of each tab, as shown in the following screenshot:

- Adding a page: Hover over a tab in the File Browser and a plus sign will appear, as shown in the following screenshot. Clicking on the plus sign will create a blank canvas page titled **New Mockup**.

- Saving a page: When a change is made to the canvas, the page tab will display an asterisk to the left of the page title, as shown in the following screenshot:

Chapter 1

To remove the asterisk, you must first save the page by selecting **File | Save**, or by pressing *Command + S* or *Ctrl + S*, on your keyboard.

> Balsamiq will not allow a page to close until it has been saved and the asterisk disappears.

- Renaming a page: Right-click on the page tab to reveal a menu of options. Select **Rename Mockup...**, as shown in the following screenshot:

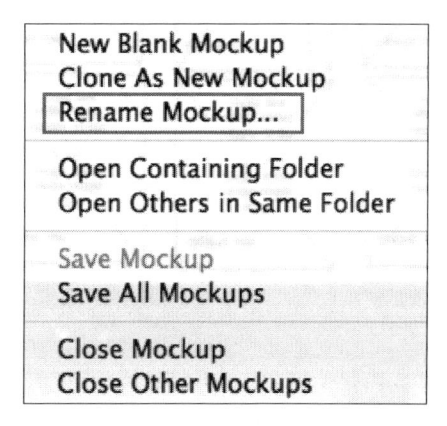

```
New Blank Mockup
Clone As New Mockup
Rename Mockup...

Open Containing Folder
Open Others in Same Folder

Save Mockup
Save All Mockups

Close Mockup
Close Other Mockups
```

Type a new filename into the text field that appears.

> Having a large number of pages open at one time can obscure their titles. When this occurs, Balsamiq automatically provides a drop-down menu at the far right of the File Browser bar.

Click on the arrow to see all of your page titles in full. Select one from the menu to bring it into view, as shown in the following screenshot:

| project... | project... | project... | * proje... | * proje... | project... | project... | symbo... | New M... | New Mockup |

[19]

Property Inspector

If you haven't already done so, drag a few elements from the UI Library onto the canvas. Once placed, click on any one of them to expose the Property Inspector, as shown in the following screenshot:

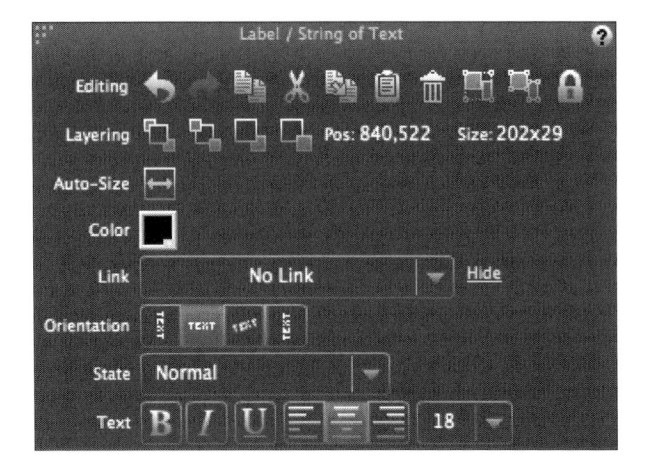

The Property Inspector is an important tool for controlling much of what happens on the canvas and is a tool you will be using very often in Balsamiq and throughout this book. As you can see in the previous screenshot, there are a number of functions that exist within the Property Inspector. Some might even look familiar to you as they work the same as in other applications.

We will explore many tools within the Property Inspector throughout this book. For now, take some time to explore your new Balsamiq backyard. And don't worry about breaking anything. It is impossible to break Balsamiq.

Summary

This brings us to the end of this chapter. By now, you will have installed Balsamiq and Adobe Air on your computer, learned about the essential tools for saving, importing and exporting files, played with the UI Library, placed elements on the canvas, opened, saved and closed pages using the File Browser, and much more.

Now that you have done all of that, take a moment to congratulate yourself. You have survived the boring stuff and can now begin to put everything you just learned into practice. In the next chapter, we will do just that and more.

Are you ready? Here we go!

2
Building a Project

In this chapter we will begin building a project. When completed, it will be yours to show off to prospective employers, colleagues, and clients alike. The material covered will also set the stage for the rest of the book, as we will cover not only wireframe design, but also design concepts often found in larger team projects, such as proper alignment, design layout, UI architecture, and how to think about your work in a larger context. The following is what we will cover in this chapter:

- The project files
- Organizing your Balsamiq files
- The project
- Alignment
- Layering
- Grouping layers
- Putting it all together

The project files

To make your job easier and to help you focus on the tasks at hand, I have provided files that I will be referring to throughout the remainder of this book. While you are free to design your own, I think you will find using the files I have provided to be an invaluable tool towards a greater understanding of Balsamiq and wireframing in general, especially if you are new to it.

> **Downloading the example code**
> You can download the example code files for all Packt books you have purchased from your account at http://www.packtpub.com. If you purchased this book elsewhere, you can visit http://www.packtpub.com/support and register to have the files e-mailed directly to you.

Building a Project

Once downloaded, you will need to unzip a file called `balsamiq_project_files`. When you open the folder, you will see a bunch of `.bmml` files—`.bmml` is the file extension that Balsamiq uses for wireframe files—and a folder called `assets`.

Organizing your Balsamiq files

There are two important things to note about organizing your files in Balsamiq:

1. Keep all of your `.bmml` files together.
2. The **assets** folder houses everything else, that is, artwork, logos, PDFs, PSDs, symbols (See *Chapter 3, Working with Symbols*), and so on, as shown in the following screenshot:

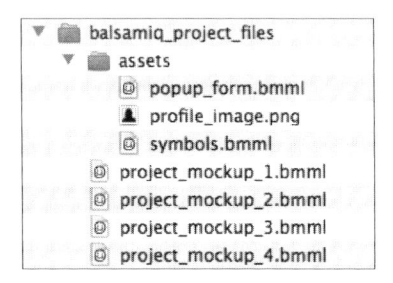

```
▼ 📁 balsamiq_project_files
    ▼ 📁 assets
            popup_form.bmml
            profile_image.png
            symbols.bmml
        project_mockup_1.bmml
        project_mockup_2.bmml
        project_mockup_3.bmml
        project_mockup_4.bmml
```

Naming your files

Naming your files in Balsamiq is very important. This is because Balsamiq does not automatically remember the order in which you organized your files after you closed them. Balsamiq will reopen them in the order in which they are sitting in a folder. There are, however, two ways you can gain greater control.

Alphabetically

You could alphabetize your files, although this could pose a problem as you add and delete files, requiring you to carefully name the new files so that they open in the same order as before.

While it is a fine solution, the time it takes to ensure proper alphabetization does not seem worth the effort.

Numbering

The second, and more productive way, to name your files is to not name them at all, but instead to number them.

For example, after naming a new `.bmml` file, add a number to the end of it in sequential order, for example, filename_1, filename_2, filename_3, and so on. Subpages, in turn, become filename_1a, filename_1b, filename_1c, and so on. Keep in mind, however, that if you add, delete, or modify numbered files, you may still have to modify the remaining page numbers accordingly. Nevertheless, I suspect you will find it to be easier than alphabetizing.

Another way to number your files can be found on Balsamiq's website. The link to the exact page is a bit long. Go to `http://www.balsamiq.com/` and do a search for `Managing Projects in Mockups for Desktop`. In the article, they recommend an alternate method of numbering your files by 10s, for example, filename_10, filename_20, filename_30, and so on. The idea being that as you add or remove pages, you can do so incrementally, rather than having to do a complete renumbering each time. In other words, you could add numbers between 11 and 19 and still be fine. Keep in mind that if you choose to use single digits, be sure to add a zero before the filename for consistency and to ensure proper file folder organization, for example, filename_05, filename_06, filename_07, and so on.

How you name or number your files is completely up to you. These tips are simply recommendations to consider. The bottom line is to find a system for naming your files that works for you and to stick with it. You will be glad you did.

The project

It is now time to build something in Balsamiq. From here onwards, you will be utilizing the files provided. You are free to build your own files too, however, the files provided will be referenced and used throughout the remainder of this book.

So what are we building?

The project is really a rebuilding, or more like an addition to a project I did for a client's SharePoint intranet portal. I chose this piece because it utilizes many of Balsamiq's tools and UI Library widgets. It also does a nice job of introducing some of the softer skills required for delivering work at a professional level, such as precise placement of elements, formatting text, building forms, information flow, and thinking in the context of a larger team, that is, handing your work off to UI developers and graphic designers. When combined, all of these elements can produce quality work, which is the real goal of this book and your goal as a wireframe designer, architect, and UI designer.

But remember, building wireframes in Balsamiq is only half the battle. The other half is about providing your team with high quality and carefully constructed, detailed work that will enable them to closely adhere to your vision and bring it to life.

Building a Project

The UI Library revisited

To begin, make sure you can see all the widgets in the UI Library. If not, click on the **All** button at the top-left of the bar, as shown in the following screenshot:

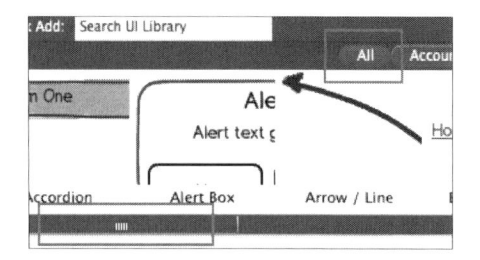

The buttons in this bar allow you to view every widget at once, or by filtering them down to their respective categories. Take the time to click through each button and familiarize yourself with how Balsamiq categorizes.

> Another way to search for widgets is to use the **Quick Add** search bar at the top of the application screen, (See *Chapter 1, Getting to know Balsamiq*). For example, start typing the word `button` into the text field, and you will see what I mean.

Adding a widget

Now, we are going to add a widget to your canvas using the files you downloaded earlier. If you haven't yet downloaded the files, now would be a good time.

With the files downloaded, perform the following steps:

1. Open the file called `project_mockup_1.bmml`.
2. Locate the widget called **Video Player** from the UI Library.

    Note that Balsamiq was kind enough to alphabetize all the widgets in the UI Library for you. In other words, **Video Player** is near the end, as shown in the following screenshot:

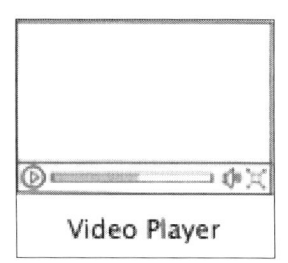

3. Drag the **Video Player** widget onto the canvas, and place it in the area marked **Place Video Player Widget Here**. Be sure to leave this text in the box. If it gets covered by the new widget, that's fine. We will refer back to it in a few moments.

First, let's position our new widget on the canvas.

Alignment

Balsamiq makes positioning easy using tools found in the Property Inspector.

To position the widget, perform the following steps:

1. Click on the **Video Player** widget to activate it.

   Doing this will make the Property Inspector appear.

2. In the second row of the inspector, called **Layering**, you will see two sets of numbers: **Pos** and **Size**, as shown in the following screenshot:

Pos represents left/right and up/down coordinates for positioning elements on the canvas. **Size** represents the elements' width and height, respectively.

With the **Video Player** widget still selected, perform the following steps:

1. Press the arrow keys on your computer keyboard in all directions.

   As you do, notice that the **Pos** numbers change with each press of the keys.

2. Click the arrows until the **Pos** numbers read: 79,260.

3. Do the same for **Size** until the numbers read: 467x216.

   If, after nudging with the arrow keys and resizing, you are unable to get to those exact numbers, there is another way to change them. Click on either set of **Pos** or **Size** numbers and these areas will become editable text fields, as shown in the following screenshot:

Building a Project

To change the numbers, simply click inside a field and begin typing. Be sure to retain the comma (**,**) for **Pos** numbers and the (**x**) between the **Size** attributes.

4. Save what you just typed by pressing *Enter/Return*, or just click anywhere outside of the text area.

5. As always, save your work.

Spend some time playing with the **Pos** and **Size** attributes, as you will use these a lot. And don't worry if you mess anything up. Balsamiq is forgiving. To return to the original settings, either make a note of what they were before you started moving things around or just hit *Command + Z/Ctrl + Z* on your keyboard as many times as necessary to return to your original settings.

Layering

Another important feature found in the Property Inspector is called **Layering**. Located in the same row as **Pos** and **Size**, layering is depicted as a series of squares, representing the different states of layer positioning, as shown in the following screenshot:

To better understand layers, just think of them as stackable objects—one layer atop the other—kind of like a sandwich with all the fixings. To see layering in action, we are once again going to add an additional element to the video section.

> The following examples refer to layering using the latest version of Balsamiq (2.1.19 as of this writing). If you are using an earlier version of Balsamiq, you will notice that the layering icons are arranged differently. I am not sure why it was changed with this latest version, but it is notable to point out nevertheless.

Perform the following steps:

1. Return to the UI Library and locate the **Webcam** widget.

2. Place it on top of the **Video Player** widget. Don't worry if it covers the text. We are going to fix that.

Chapter 2

If you deleted the text, just grab any other widget from the UI Library and add it to your stack so that you have a total of three widgets.

To rearrange the layers, perform the following steps:

1. Click on the **Webcam** widget to activate it. (That's the box with the smiley face).
2. In the Property Inspector, click the **Layering** icon that is third from the left, as shown in the following screenshot:

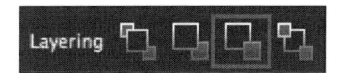

This tool is also known as the **Send Backward** button. If you are using an older version of Balsamiq, this icon is positioned second from the left.

> You may have to click the **Send Backward** button twice to activate it. If nothing seems to happen just play around with the other buttons until it looks like the image shown in the following screenshot.

If successful, that line of text should now appear above the **Video widget**, as shown in the following screenshot:

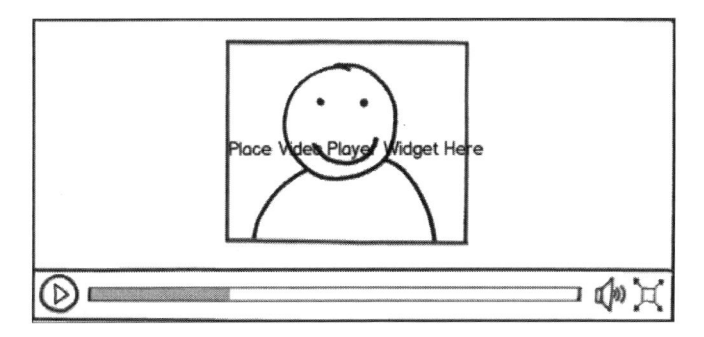

[27]

For a closer look at layering, here is a description of the four tools, as per the order in which they appear in the Property Inspector, for Balsamiq v2.1.19:

- **Bring to Front**: The selected element is sent immediately to the top of the stack.
- **Bring Forward**: The selected element moves forward in the stack one layer at a time. The more you click, the higher up the element moves in the stack.
- **Send Backward**: The selected element moves one layer at a time down the layer stack until it hits the bottom.
- **Send to Back**: The selected element is sent immediately to the bottom of the stack.

You will find that it takes practice and some trial and error before you master layers. Keep at it though. Although there may be some frustration and/or confusion early on, it will all begin to make sense soon enough.

Grouping layers

As you become more comfortable with Balsamiq, you will begin to add many widgets and layers to your wireframes. You will find that moving multiple widgets around the page can be tricky. To make it easy, you first have to group them.

Perform the following steps:

1. Using your mouse and pressing *Shift*, click on the elements you want as part of your group. You can also drag around the area that you want to group.
2. With your desired set of elements selcted, press *Command + G/Ctrl + G* or choose **Group** from the **Edit** menu.

Notice that the selected elements change color to indicate that they are now grouped. You can now move the entire group around the canvas, as shown in the following screenshot:

To ungroup, press *Command + Shift + G* or select **Ungroup** from the **Edit** menu at the top of your screen.

> Sometimes, not all the elements are successfully selected. For example, if you drag around a group of elements to select them and one is not shaded then that item is not selected. To fix it, press the *Shift* key and click on the item again. Once it becomes shaded, you will know it is successfully selected.
>
> You can also select everything on the canvas by pressing: *Command + A / Ctrl + A*.

Putting it all together

Now it's time to review what you have learned. We will do this by adding a new section to your wireframe, indicated with an arrow in the following screenshot:

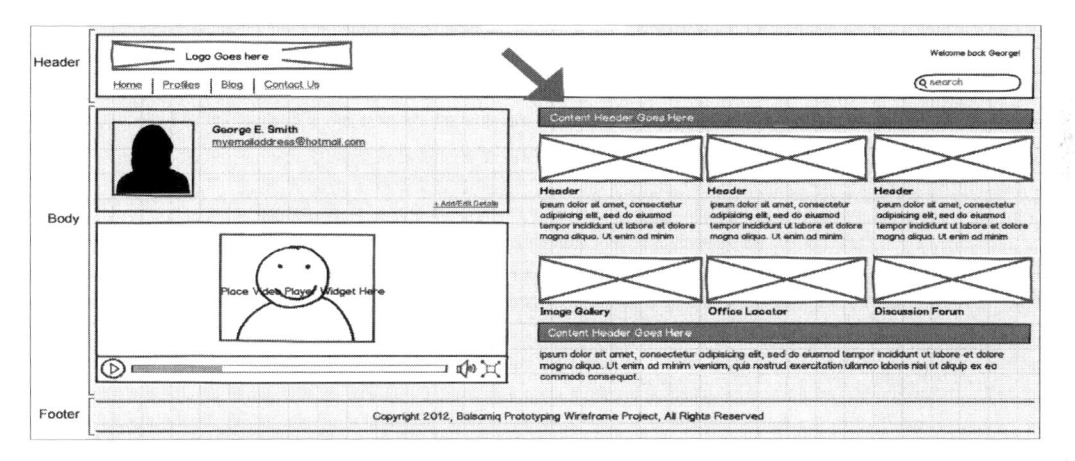

Before we begin: A brief word about design and layout

You will notice that the completed wireframe in the previous screenshot consists of essentially three main areas. There is the Header for logo and navigation, the Body for personal info, video, and a section for content and images. Lastly, there is the Footer showing the copyright information.

Taken separately, these are all very important pieces of your design. Taken together, they can make or break the experience of your users if not laid out correctly. Remember, good design and proper balance should never be taken for granted.

Building a Project

As you walk through this chapter, and as you build your wireframe, take note of the symmetry and flow of the designs presented. The alignment of elements to each other, their exact positioning and the way information flows from top-down and left to right are key factors to consider and follow for good design. When you send your work off for coding or to the design team to turn into hi-fidelity screens, you will often find that your work is taken very literally. If you take the time to design with attention to detail you can lead your design team towards a professional, high quality product that your end users will greatly appreciate and that you can be proud of.

While this book does not cover these very important topics, I do offer some great resources in *Chapter 7, Parting Thoughts: Resources and Recommendations*, that will help you to become more attuned to these factors and how to use them to your advantage.

Knowing how to wireframe is essential. Knowing how to design great user experiences is equally important. Learn them and you will be well on your way to great results.

Rectangle/Canvas/Panel

Let's begin by creating what we will call the section headers. These will be used to divide the sections of text and images, as shown in the example.

The following is what the completed section header will look like:

[Content Header Goes Here]

To build it, perform the following steps:

1. Find the widget named **Rectangle/Canvas/Panel** in the UI Library. You can also search for it using **Quick Search** or by clicking on the **Common** button atop the UI Library.
2. Place the widget onto the canvas and position it: **Pos:** `578,111`.
3. Size it as well: **Size:** `562x29`.

Next, we will change the color of the section header:

1. Click on the **Rectangle/Canvas/Panel** so it is selected.
2. With the Property Inspector visible, click on the left most color square to open the color palette.

[30]

3. In the palette, locate the fourth color square from the left, in the top row. Click on it to change the color of the panel, as shown in the following screenshot:

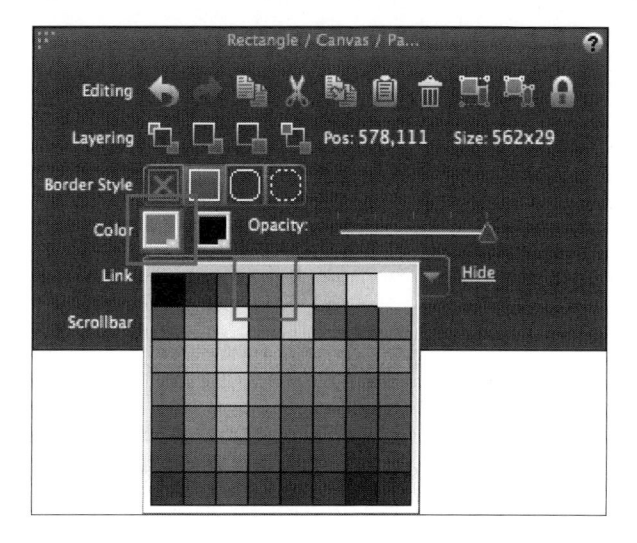

The area header should now be shaded using the color you chose. You can also control the opacity of the color using the slider to the right. Opacity is the level of transparency given to your colors. For this exercise, we are keeping the opacity at its default of 100 percent.

Adding text

While we do not discuss text until *Chapter 5, Icons, Images, and Text*, I thought I would give you a preview to help complete this exercise. Perform the following steps:

1. Locate the widget in the UI Library called **Label/String of Text** and drop it onto your newly created section header.
2. With the text widget selected, press *Return/Enter* on your keyboard, or double-click on it to make it editable. Type in `Content Header Goes Here`.
3. Click outside the box to close it.
4. Position the textbox: **Pos:** `589,115`.
5. Save your work.

Your section header should now look like the following screenshot:

Building a Project

To change the text color, perform the following steps:

1. Click on the color box once again in the Property Inspector and select the white square (It is the furthest square in the top row).
2. Select the text box and the section header rectangle and group them.
3. Position the group: **Pos:** 578,111.
4. Make a duplicate (Copy/Paste).
5. Position the duplicate group: **Pos:** 578,394.

Your screen should now look like the following screenshot:

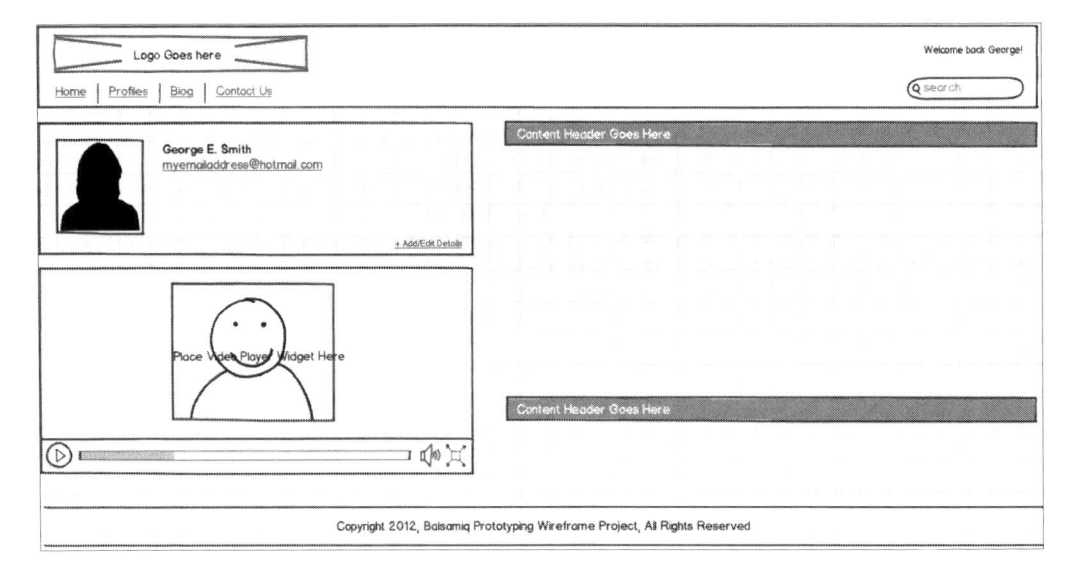

Images

Now, we are going to place some image widgets on the canvas:

1. Locate the **Image** widget in the UI Library and place it on the canvas.
2. Size it: **Size:** 185x64.
3. Now, drag two more **Image** widgets onto the canvas and position them horizontally near the first one.

Don't worry about exact positioning just yet. First, we are going to do some aligning.

[32]

Align tool

In addition to positioning, the Property Inspector also offers useful tools for aligning widgets and groups to each other on the canvas.

Now let's try that by performing the following steps:

1. Select the left-most **Image** widget and the section header above it.
2. In the Property Inspector, select the first tool in the **Align** row called **Align Left**, as shown in the following screenshot:

Once clicked, the two elements will become left aligned to each other, as shown in the following screenshot:

For this example to work correctly, the section header should be the left-most object. Since you already positioned the section header earlier, use it as your guide and align the **Image** widget to it.

Now let's align this **Image** widget to the other two by performing the following steps:

1. Select all three **Image** widgets.
2. Click the **Align Top** tool (fourth from the left) to top-align all three widgets to each other, as shown in the following screenshot:

3. Finally, space them evenly using the **Align Middle** tool, as shown in the following screenshot:

[33]

Building a Project

As stated previously, be sure that the left-most **Image** widget remains left aligned to the section header.

Your screen should now look something like the following screenshot:

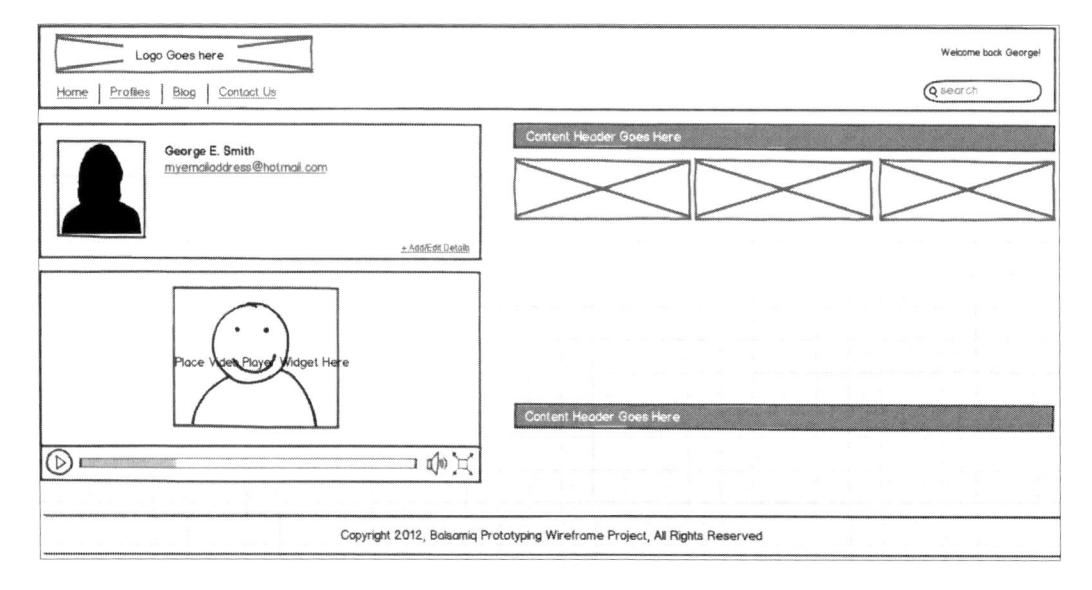

Once that's completed, do the following:

1. Grab all three **Image** widgets and group them.
2. Copy and paste to make a duplicate group.
3. Position the duplicate group: **Pos:** `578,306`.

Fool around with positioning and alignment and get comfortable with using them. This may take some practice, but then that's why we're here, right?

The body copy

By now, you may have noticed some copy on the right-hand side of the canvas. This was provided for you to use as part of this exercise. In reality, it is just some random dummy copy I created to save you the time of typing it yourself. But don't worry. You will have plenty of time to create your own text in *Chapter 5, Icons, Images, and Text*.

For now, click anywhere on or near the text to select it. To save you some time, it is already grouped. You just need to position it: **Pos:** `578,211`.

If you prefer, you can also ungroup the text and play around with it. For example, you could move stuff around using the positioning tools, play with the alignment tools, add some text of your own or play with the layer tools in the Property Inspector. When you are done, group it again and reposition the text so it looks like the finished wireframe in the example. You can also click *Command + Z/Ctrl + Z* as many times as needed to get it back to its original state.

Your final screen should look like the following screenshot:

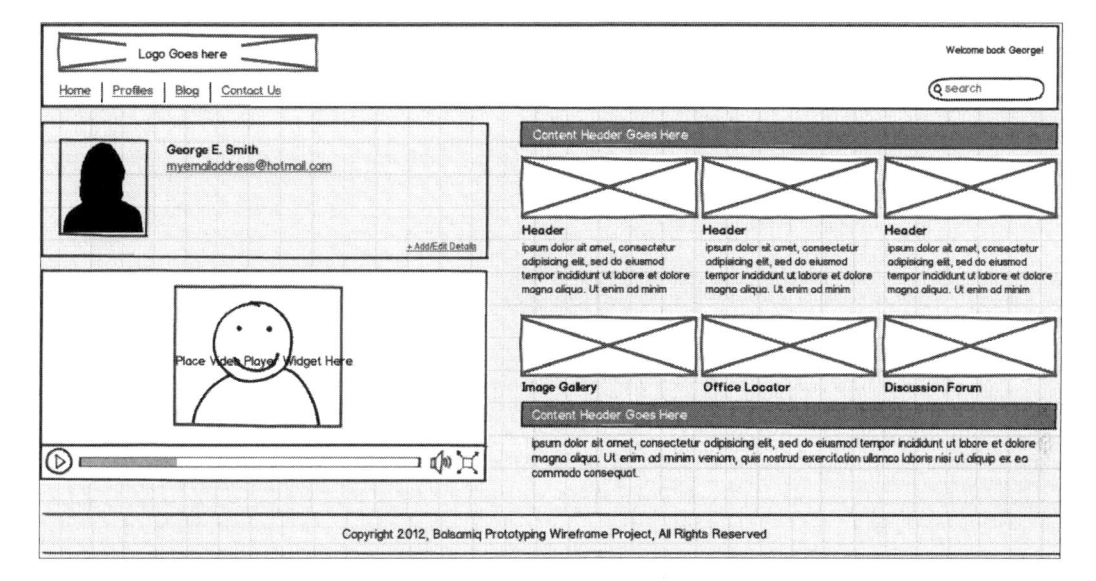

Summary

So how did you do? Does your wireframe match the sample? Did you add some elements of your own? No matter what you ended up with, I hope you found it to be a fun and easy experience. With Balsamiq, it is often both.

We covered a lot in this chapter. You were introduced to the project and downloaded the files we will use throughout the remainder of this book. We also walked through important aspects of Balsamiq and UI design in general, such as organizing your files, naming them, positioning elements on the page, working with layers, and grouping.

As we move on to the next chapter, you will begin to add yet another layer of complexity to your wireframes as we delve into symbols and into creating your own custom widgets.

Ready? Set? Let's go!

3
Working with Symbols

Now, we are going to get into some more complexity by introducing a key Balsamiq feature, known as symbols.

The following list shows what we will cover in this chapter:

- What are symbols?
- Creating a symbol
- Modifying a symbol
- Revisiting the wireframe project
- Creating a symbol library
- Sharing symbols

What are symbols?

In the previous chapter, we introduced grouping as a useful way to keep your widgets together on the canvas and reusing those same groups across multiple pages by copy-pasting them. Another type of grouping used in Balsamiq is called symbols. Like groups, symbols give you the ability to reuse elements across your entire wireframe project. The difference is, symbols are more similar to master pages, where a change to a single file can cascade throughout an entire project.

That may sound complicated, but it will all become very clear by the time you complete this chapter.

Working with Symbols

Creating a symbol

To create a symbol, there are just a few steps to take, a few new tools to learn, and a few important things to remember. So, let's dive right in by turning one of the elements already in your wireframe project into a symbol. Perform the following steps for doing so:

1. If it's not already open, select `project_mockup_1.bmml` from the `balsamiq_project_files` folder and open it.

2. Select all the elements in the header area by clicking-and-dragging the mouse around the entire section, as shown in the following screenshot:

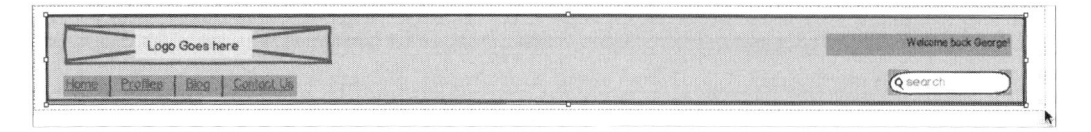

   You can also select by pressing *Shift* while clicking on each piece of the header.

3. Once everything is selected, turn the header into a group, by pressing *Command* + *G*/*Ctrl* + *G*.

4. The Property Inspector will appear, indicating that it is now a **Group**, as shown in the following screenshot:

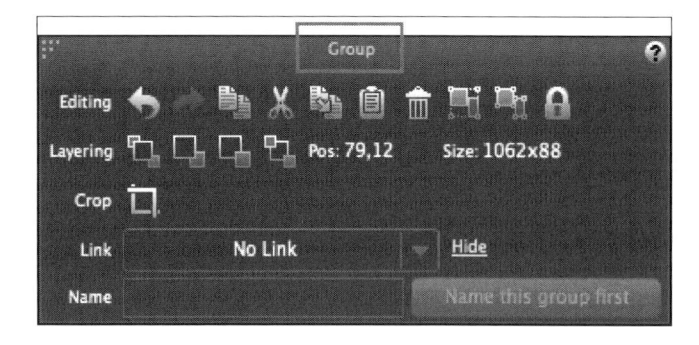

5. Give your new group a name by typing it into the **Name** textbox in the Property Inspector. For example, you can name it `wireframe_header`, as shown in the following screenshot:

[38]

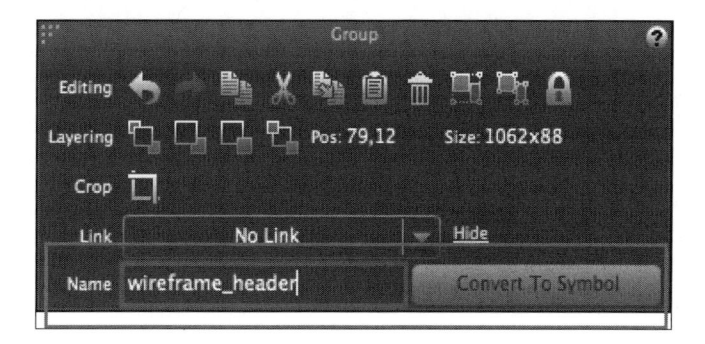

6. When you type in the **Name** field, notice that the button next to it changes from **Name this group first** to **Convert To Symbol**.
7. When you are done typing, click on the **Convert To Symbol** button. Once clicked, your grouping will turn green, indicating that it is now a symbol.

> By changing this group into a symbol, you have modified the page. In other words, remember to save your work.

Location of the saved symbols

Now that you have created your first symbol, you might be wondering where did Balsamiq put it? Luckily, Balsamiq puts your symbols in a unique and easy-to-find place where you have easy access to them anytime.

To find it, select the **Project Assets** button from the UI Library. **Project Assets** is where Balsamiq stores all of your symbols, as shown in the following screenshot:

You should now see the newly created **wireframe_header** symbol in the project assets bar, as shown in the following screenshot:

[39]

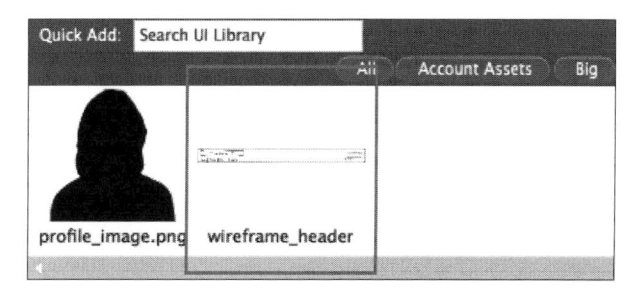

Symbols.bmml

While Balsamiq makes finding your symbols easy using the UI Library, there is one other place where symbols are kept.

Perform the following steps to find it:

1. Open the `balsamiq_project_files` folder.
2. Once inside, open the `assets` folder.

There you will find a file called `symbols.bmml`. Open this file to find the symbol you have just created.

Symbols as a master page

To understand symbols better, think of `symbols.bmml` as a "master page". For those not familiar with the term, a **master page** is an individual page where common elements, such as a header, footer, navigation, and so on—that is, things that are shared across multiple pages in your project—can be placed. Make a change to the master page and those changes will cascade throughout your entire project, saving you from having to make those same changes page by page.

We will do an exercise later so that you can see this in action.

> For the record, Balsamiq does not refer to this view as a "master page". I am calling it that to give you a clearer vision of what this page essentially is.

Modifying a symbol

Making changes to a symbol is easy, but there are a few ways to do it. We will look at them in a moment.

Page by page

This method will allow you to make changes to a symbol on a page-by-page basis. For example, open `project_mockup_1.bmml` and double-click on the header.

You should now see a green bar across the top of the canvas, as shown in the following screenshot:

> 🏠 ▸ Overiding properties of control #83 (wireframe_header)

In this state, your symbol is fully editable, but any changes you make will apply only to this particular instance.

> The number in the green bar (**#83** in this example), is an ID number that Balsamiq creates automatically. This number becomes part of the page's file data and can be referenced during development, if needed. While developing with Balsamiq is outside the scope of this book, I thought you might want to know.

All pages

To change a symbol across multiple pages, you have to look at the other side of the green bar and click on the **Edit** button, as shown in the following screenshot:

> Want to edit the symbol source instead? **Edit**

Clicking on **Edit** brings you to the master page—`symbols.bmml` where, once again, your symbol is fully editable. However, any changes you make here will cascade throughout your entire project.

Let's try an exercise. Perform the following steps:

1. Open `project_mockup_2.bmml` and drag the header symbol from the **Project Assets** bar. Set **Pos**: `79,12`.
2. Return to `symbols.bmml` and select the text in the upper-right area of the header, where it says **Welcome back George!**, as shown in the following screenshot:

> Logo Goes here   Welcome back George!
> Home | Profiles | Blog | Contact Us   search

3. Change **George** to your name.

   If your name happens to be George, well, sorry George. For this exercise, please choose a different name.
4. Save your work for the changes to take effect.
5. Return to `project_mockup_2.bmml` and notice that the name in the header has changed. Notice that it also changed in `project_mockup_1.bmml`.
6. To remove the green bar, double-click anywhere on the page or press the *Esc* key on your keyboard.

Working with Symbols

Additional ways to edit a symbol

Select the header in `project_mockup_2.bmml` once more to make the Property Inspector visible. Once there, you will see two buttons at the bottom, **Break Apart** and **Edit Source**, within the row labeled **Symbol**, as shown in the following screenshot:

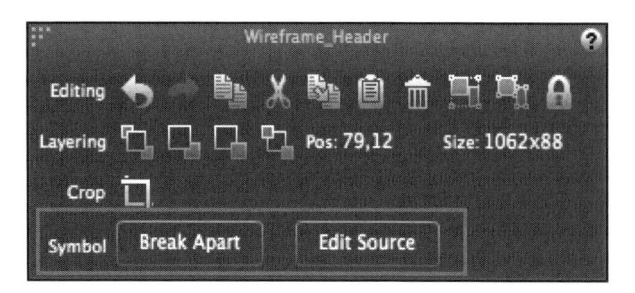

Break Apart

Clicking on the **Break Apart** button turns a symbol back into a group and essentially disconnects it from the master page. At this point, the only way to turn it back into a symbol is to rename it and create a new symbol or, if you did this by mistake, you can always press *Command* + *Z*/*Ctrl* + *Z* until it is returned to its original symbol state.

Edit Source

Edit Source brings you back to the master page—`symbols.bmml`. From here, you can edit the symbol as before with all changes cascading throughout your project.

Project Assets

A third way to edit can be found in the UI Library's **Project Assets** section. Just right-click on the symbol icon and click on **Edit Symbol Source**. This will take you back to the master page, `symbols.bmml`, once again.

Reverting to saved

Before moving on, there is one other useful feature for editing symbols that you should know about as well.

[42]

It is easier to show you this one directly using an example. Perform the following steps:

1. Open `project_mockup_2.bmml` and double-click on the header once again to activate the green bar.
2. With the green bar visible, make some changes to the header. Any change will do.
3. Close the green bar (double-click on the canvas or click *Esc*).
4. Reselect the header.

You should now see something similar to the following screenshot in the Property Inspector:

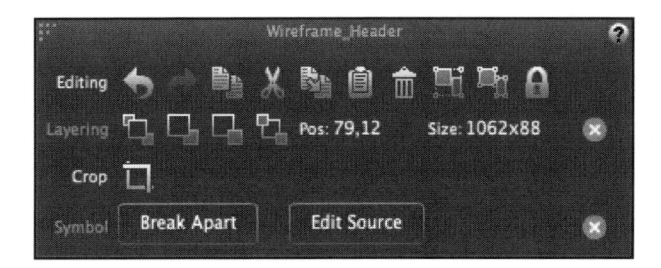

Notice the green **x** icons on the right side of the Property Inspector. They alert you that something has changed in the symbol on this page that is different from the master page version. Clicking on either of the green **x** icons will remove any changes you made and return the header to its previous master page version.

On the other hand, if you are happy with your changes, save your work and the green **x** icons will disappear.

Deleting a symbol

Deleting a symbol is, of course, just as easy as creating one and there are two ways to accomplish this. We will look at them in a moment.

Page by page

Delete a symbol on the page you are on. This will delete the symbol on that page only.

All pages

Delete a symbol via the master page, `symbols.bmml`. Doing so will delete every instance of the symbol throughout your entire project.

Revisiting the wireframe project

It is time to put your newly acquired knowledge of symbols to good use. We will do this by adding a header symbol to the remaining pages of your wireframe project and adding a brand new symbol to the footer as well. Perform the following steps for doing so:

1. Open the `balsamiq_project_files` folder, which houses all of your project files.
2. Select all the `.bmml` files sitting outside of the `assets` folder, as shown in the screenshot just after the following information box.

> Check the page ordering in your folder before opening your files, as they will open in that exact order in Balsamiq.

The correct order is as follows:

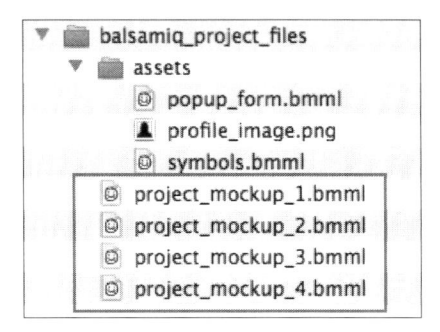

```
▼ balsamiq_project_files
  ▼ assets
      popup_form.bmml
      profile_image.png
      symbols.bmml
    project_mockup_1.bmml
    project_mockup_2.bmml
    project_mockup_3.bmml
    project_mockup_4.bmml
```

If you are using Macintosh, you can open multiple files by selecting them and then right-clicking on the selected area. In the menu that appears, choose Open. Another option is to select the files and double-click anywhere on the selected group.

Adding symbols to multiple pages

With all of your pages opened, let's place the header onto every page. There are three ways to do this. We will look at them in a moment.

Copying and pasting the symbol

As we have placed the header symbol onto two pages already, let's start there. Perform the following steps:

1. Select `project_mockup_2.bmml`.
2. Click on the header.
3. Press *Command* + *C*/*Ctrl* + *C* to copy it to the clipboard.
4. Select `project_mockup_3.bmml` from the file browser.
5. Paste the header symbol onto the page by pressing *Command* + *V*/*Ctrl* + *V*.
6. Position it as **Pos**: `79,12`.
7. Repeat steps 2 to 6 on every other page.

> Balsamiq is generally pretty good about pasting elements into their correct location on a new page. Nevertheless, remember to double-check the positioning each time you paste something, just to be sure.

8. Finally, save your work!

After completing this exercise, it is a good opportunity to use the **Save All** functionality in the **File** menu, as you need to save the changes made to every page. Save yourself some time. Try it!

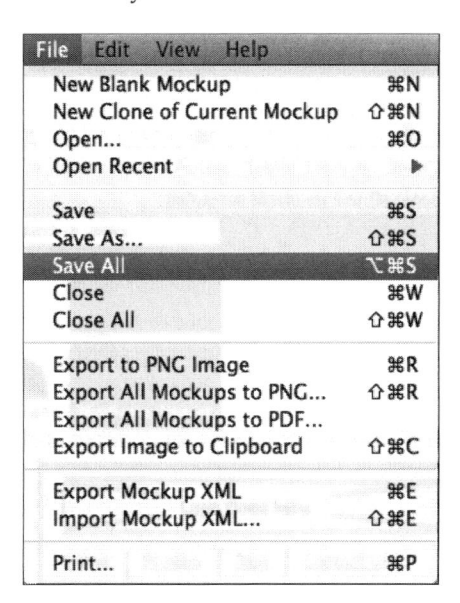

Working with Symbols

Dragging the symbol

The second way to add a symbol to a page is to drag it onto each page from **Project Assets** in the UI Library.

Double-clicking on the symbol

Lastly, double-click on a symbol in the **Project Assets** bar in the UI Library to place it on your canvas. Be sure to check its positioning.

Creating a new symbol

Now let's create a brand new symbol. This will become the copyright line at the bottom of every page. Perform the following steps:

1. Select `project_mockup_1.bmml`.
2. Click on the **Layout** button in the UI Library.
3. Find the widget called **Horizontal Rule** and drag it two times to the bottom of the canvas.
4. Make both horizontal lines of equal width: **Size**: `1063x5`.
5. Align them by clicking on the **Align Left** icon in the Property Inspector's **Align** tools (If you recall, it is the first tool in the row).
6. Group them.
7. Position the group as **Pos**: `79,576`.

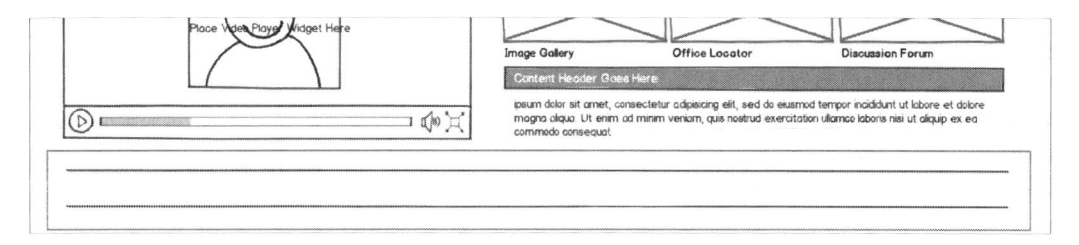

Adding some text

Let's add some footer text by performing the following steps:

1. Click on the **Text** button in the UI Library.
2. Select **Label/String of Text** and drag it to the bottom of the canvas, in between the horizontal lines.
3. Size it as **Size**: `1063x21`.

[46]

4. Position it as **Pos**: `79,588`.
5. Type `Copyright 2012, Balsamiq Prototyping Wireframe Project, All Rights Reserved`.
6. Center the text using the **Align Center** text tool in the Property Inspector, as shown in the following screenshot:

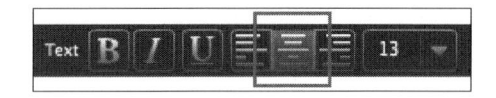

7. Group the text and the two lines.
8. In the Property Inspector, name the group as `copyright_footer`.
9. Click on the **Convert to** Symbol.
10. Save your work!

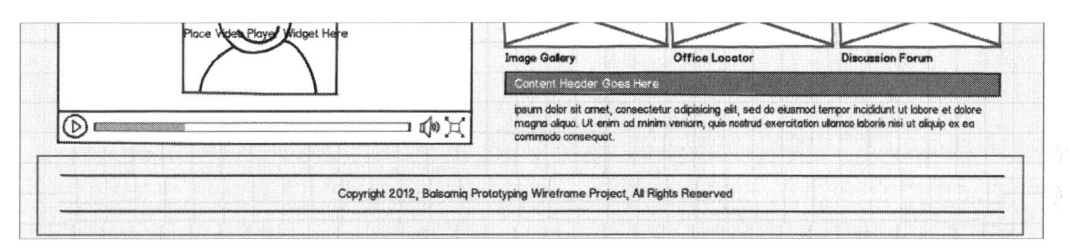

Although you are naming each of your symbols differently, Balsamiq puts all of them into one `symbols.bmml` page. This can come in handy when you start building symbol libraries, which we will talk about next.

Adding the footer to all pages

Place your new copyright symbol at the bottom of every page. Remember to position them correctly, **Pos**: `79,576`, and to select **Save All** when you are done.

Great work! Your wireframe is really starting to take shape.

Creating a symbol library

When you return to `symbols.bmml`, you will see that Balsamiq has placed both the header and the footer symbols on the same page. While it may look crowded, this is actually a useful feature.

Working with Symbols

To demonstrate, I am going to share with you a very cool website that I am sure you will thank me for later. Please type the following address into your web browser:

`https://mockupstogo.mybalsamiq.com/projects`

Once at this web address, in the **All Public Projects** section, scroll to the section titled **Social**. Once there, perform the following steps:

1. On the **Social** page, find the wireframe called **Blog Post**. This wireframe has been created by Michael Angeles using Balsamiq Mockups.
2. Click the small, downward-facing arrow next to the title.
3. Select **Download BMML**, as shown in the following screenshot:

4. Place the `.bmml` file you just downloaded, `Blog Post.bmml`, into your project's `assets` folder.

Adding the symbol to your project

Let's take a closer look at your new symbol library by adding it to a page in your wireframe project. Perform the following steps:

1. Select `project_mockup_3.bmml`.
2. Drag the **Blog Post** symbol from **Project Assets** onto the canvas.
3. Position it as **Pos**: `79,117`.

4. If it's not already there, drag a header symbol onto the page.
5. Position it as **Pos**: `79,12`.
6. Drag a footer symbol onto the page.
7. Position it as **Pos**: `79,1072`.
8. Save your work!

The following screenshot shows what your page should look like:

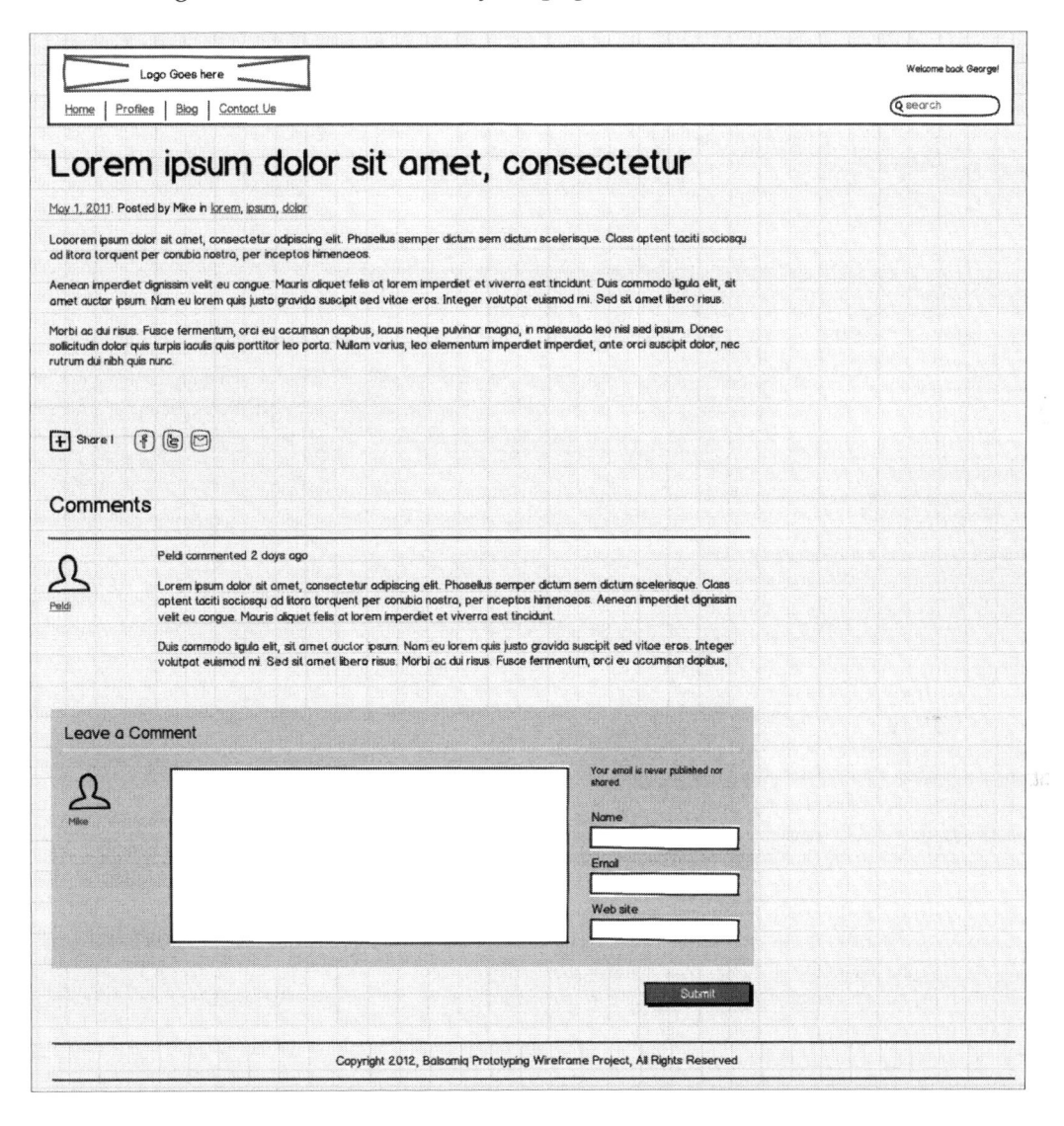

Working with Symbols

To reuse only some of the elements of a symbol library, either copy and paste the items you need from the master page, symbols.bmml, or override the symbol library on an individual page and delete or edit from there.

Sharing symbols

Now that you have created symbols and symbol libraries, you might want to share them across multiple projects. If so, you are in luck! There are two easy ways to do this with Balsamiq. We will look at them in a moment.

Project by project

If you want to share your symbols on a project-by-project basis, perform the following steps:

1. Copy symbols.bmml from the assets folder of your current project.
2. Place the copy into the assets folder of another project.

> You cannot have two symbols.bmml files in an assets folder. If you are copying a file called symbols.bmml to another assets folder, which already has one, you can just rename the new file.

All projects

Suppose you want to share a symbol library across multiple projects. No problem! Perform the following steps for doing so:

1. Locate the Documents folder on your computer's hard drive.
2. Once there, locate the folder called Balsamiq Mockups.

   This folder was automatically created when you installed Balsamiq. If for some reason you don't see it, you will need to create one for this to work.

   Once inside this folder, perform the following steps:

3. Locate the assets subfolder. Similarly, if you don't see an assets subfolder, you must create one for this to work.
4. Place symbols.bmml or whatever you named your symbol file, into the assets folder, as shown in the following screenshot:

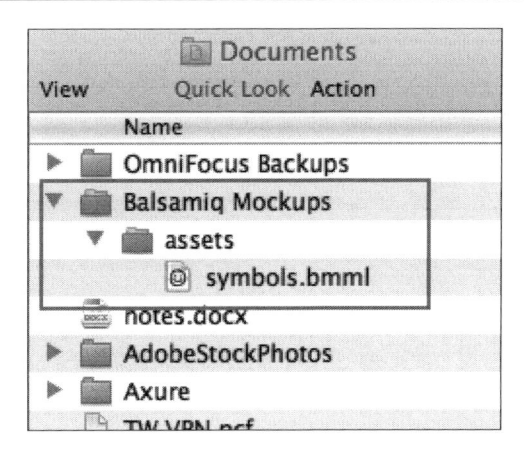

When you return to Balsamiq, you will see a new button in the UI Library called **Account Assets**. Click on it to view your new global symbol library. This library will now appear in every wireframe that you create.

If you want to delete it, simply delete the file from **Documents** | **Balsamiq Mockups** | **assets**.

It's really that simple!

Summary

As you have learned, symbols are a unique way to share widgets across an entire wireframe project and across wireframes of multiple projects. They are also useful, in that, you can create master pages and change things across an entire project by editing a single file. In addition, you learned how to find and use symbol libraries and what that can do for your productivity. Symbols are a powerful way to take control of your Balsamiq wireframes and can make a large project much easier to manage and more efficient.

In the next chapter, we will get into a whole new area of Balsamiq by introducing data grids, tables, building web forms, and how to provide UI developers with guidelines for the larger team to follow and understand your specifications.

So if you are ready, turn the page and let's continue.

4
Building Data Tables

In the previous chapter, you were introduced to symbols, which allow you to take greater control of your wireframes. In this chapter, we will continue to build on that theme as we introduce data tables into your wireframe design, turning data into useful, interactive, and engaging experiences for our end users.

The following list shows what we will cover in this chapter:

- Data tables
- Formatting data
- Deciphering the data
- Data table tips
- Wireframe project revisited
- Even more tips

Data tables

For many Internet users, data tables can seem like the online equivalent of Excel spreadsheets. They are often dull, hard to read, and more often than not full of useful data that users want and need in order to do their jobs more effectively.

Yes, data tables are actually very useful tools for relaying information to users. But like Excel, data tables can go unnoticed and ignored simply because they are not formatted with the end user in mind.

But, building data tables does not have to be a dull or complicated experience. In fact, it can, and should, be an interactive one where users not only get the information they need, but where they can also take action on the data, making it more useful to them as a result.

Building Data Tables

Now, before we dig any deeper, let's start with the basics. Perform the following steps:

1. Open `project_mockup_4.bmml`.

    If you have been following along up until this point in the book, the canvas should already have a header and footer in place. If not, please add them.

2. In the **Quick Add** search field, type the word `data`.

3. Select **Data Grid/Table**, as shown in the following screenshot:

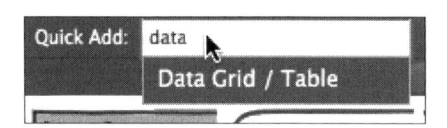

    Once selected, a data table will appear on the canvas.

    > Although I refer to them as data tables, they can also be called data grids. I simply made a decision as to what to call them for the purposes of writing this book, but either of them is correct.

    Let's position the data table and change its size.

4. Set **Size:** `1062x468`.
5. Set **Pos:** `79,100`.

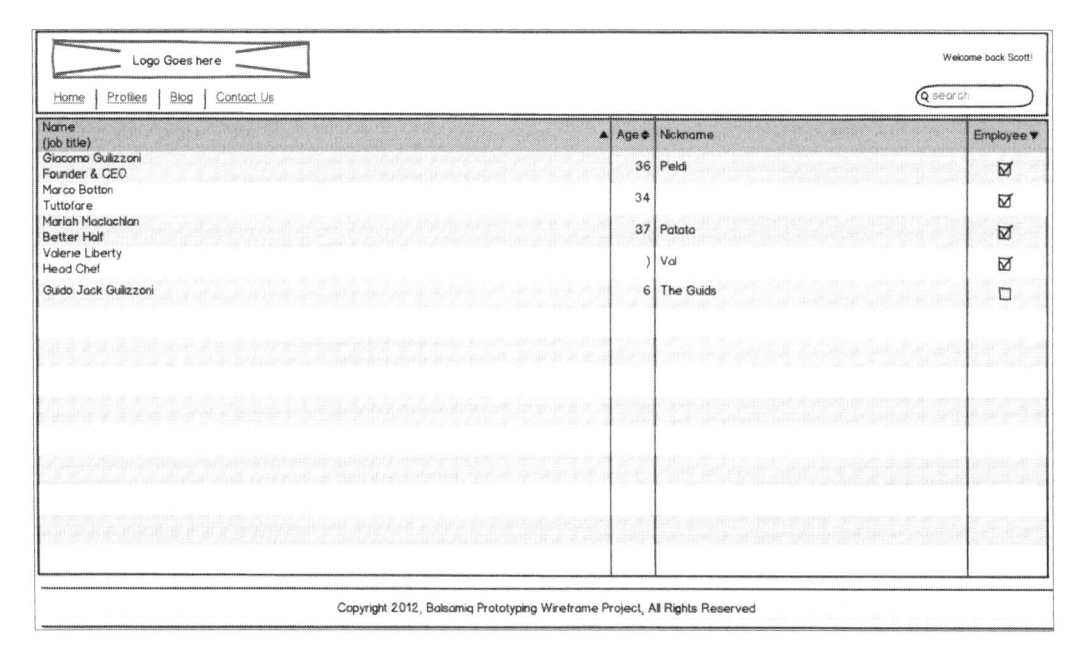

[54]

Formatting data

You may have noticed that your new data table is already filled with data. The reason for this is simple. Balsamiq requires very specific formatting for data tables. The pre-filled data is simply a guide to help you get started. Nevertheless, there is still a lot to cover.

To begin, double-click the data table to bring it into edit mode. Your table will now look like the following screenshot:

```
Name\r(job title) ^, Age ^v, Nickname, Employee v
Giacomo Guilizzoni\rFounder & CEO, 36, Peldi, [x]
Marco Botton\rTuttofare, 34, , [x]
Mariah Maclachlan\rBetter Half, 37, Patata, [x]
Valerie Liberty\rHead Chef, :), Val, [x]
Guido Jack Guilizzoni, 6, The Guids, []
{65L, 0R, 35, 0C}
```

As you can see from the previous screenshot, there is a lot going on. But while it might look like a jumbled mess at first glance, it is really quite organized.

Deciphering the data

Before we get into the details of the data, let's take a moment to review the basic data table structure.

If you are not familiar with using data tables, there are two important things to remember: rows run top to bottom and columns run left to right, as shown in the following screenshot:

	Col 1	Col 2	Col 3	Col 4
Row 1	Name (job title)	Age	Nickname	Employee ▼
Row 2	Giacomo Guilizzoni Founder & CEO	36	Peldi	☑
Row 3	Marco Botton Tuttofare	34		☑
Row 4	Mariah Maclachlan Better Half	37	Patata	☑
Row 5	Valerie Liberty Head Chef	:)	Val	☑
Row 6	Guido Jack Guilizzoni	6	The Guids	☐

Building Data Tables

While it is a bit hard to see in edit mode, the rows and columns are still there. You just have to know how to look for them, as shown in the following screenshot:

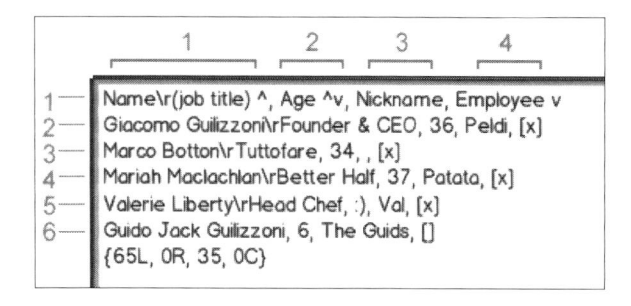

Columns and rows: A closer look

In edit mode, creating columns is as simple as adding commas between words, as shown in the following screenshot:

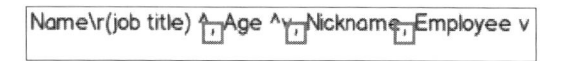

Removing columns is just as easy. Simply delete the commas.

> While somewhat hidden, the *Tab* key provides the same functionality as adding commas. However, I would recommend sticking to comma usage as it provides much better visual clarity while in edit mode.

Pressing *Return/Enter* on your keyboard creates rows. In Balsamiq, the very first row is automatically designated as the table header. You can recognize the header because it is more darkly shaded than the other rows, as shown in the following screenshot:

Grid form elements

In addition to the text, you will also notice some odd looking symbols, such as \r, ^, [x], []. Don't be alarmed. Balsamiq uses these as unique, but effective ways of formatting the data, as shown in the following screenshot:

[56]

Chapter 4

```
Name\r(job title) ^, Age ^v Nickname, Employee v
Giacomo Guilizzoni\rFounder & CEO, 36, Peldi, [x]
Marco Bottan\rTuttofare, 34, , [x]
Mariah Maclachlan\rBetter Half, 37, Patata, [x]
Valerie Liberty\rHead Chef, :), Val, [x]
Guido Jack Guilizzoni, 6, The Guids []
{65L, 0R, 35, 0C}
```

Let's take a closer look:

- (\r): Creates a line break
- (^) *Shift + 6*: Displays a sorting/filtering arrow, ascending

   Used only in the header; these are used to depict arrows normally used in data tables to toggle data from top to bottom.

- (v): Displays a sorting/filtering arrow, descending

   It is similar to the previous symbol, but is downward facing.

- [x]: Displays a checked form checkbox
- []: Displays an unchecked form checkbox
- () *Shift + 9 + Shift + 0*: Displays an unselected radio button
- (o) *Shift + 9 + o + Shift + 0*: Displays a selected radio button

> There may be times when you need to display large, comma delimited, numbers in your data table's columns. Since commas create columns, you must place a backslash just after the number, followed by a comma. For example, if you wanted to display the numbers 1, 2, 3, you would type 1\, 2\, 3. 5,000 would be 5\,000, and so on.

Width and alignment controls

While the first row designates the data table header, the last row is reserved for controlling the width of your table's columns, the text alignment within them, and the number of columns, as shown in the following screenshot:

```
Valerie Liberty\rHead Chef, :), Val, [x]
Guido Jack Guilizzoni, 6, The Guids, []
{65L, 0R, 35, 0C}
```

Building Data Tables

To understand how to use these correctly, there are some important things to remember such as the following:

- Your data table must be in the edit mode to use the number/letter functionality
- These numbers/letters must always go in the very last row in your data table
- All number/letter combinations must be placed in curly brackets
- Column width can be either relative or absolute

    In Balsamiq, relative and absolute measurement is not perfect. However, you will find them to be more than adequate for the purposes of wireframing.

- 0 is the smallest number you can use to control the width

    0 is generally used to create very narrow column widths, often reserved for data that doesn't take up a lot of space, like zip codes, yes/no responses, checkboxes, a person's age, and so on.

- Letters next to numbers assign the text alignment

> In our current data table example, {65L, 0R, 35, 0C}, the coordinates tell us that the table will have four columns. The first column is 65 percent wide with left-aligned text. The second coordinate creates a column as small as possible with right-aligned text. The third column is 35 percent wide with no text alignment assigned. The fourth coordinate creates a column as small as possible, but centers the text within it. Omitting an alignment setting, as in column three, will default its text to be left-aligned.

Lastly, single digits control the relative width. For example, {2L, 1R} will create two columns, the first, 2L, being twice as big as the second with left-aligned text. The second column, 1R, is half the width of the first column with right-aligned text.

If you choose not to supply a letter alongside a width coordinate, you can still control its alignment using the **Text** alignment tool in the Property Inspector. Just note that any columns not formally assigned a letter will all move in the same direction when using this tool.

All that sounds like quite a lot to remember, but once you start using these data table controls and coordinates regularly, you will find them to be quite intuitive.

Data table tips

When designing a wireframe, you want your design to be as close to real life as possible. Although wireframes have their limitations, Balsamiq offers a few tricks that allow you to do just that.

Highlighting a table row

Use this feature when you want to show a data table row as being selected.

Perform the following steps:

1. Click on the data table to make it active.
2. In the Property Inspector, locate the **Selection** menu, as shown in the following screenshot:

3. Click the arrow on the right to expose a list of every row in your data table.
4. Select one of the rows, as shown in the following screenshot:

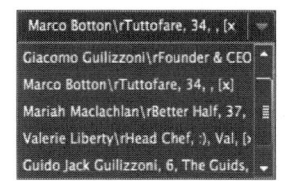

5. Deselect the data table and see the results, as shown in the following screenshot:

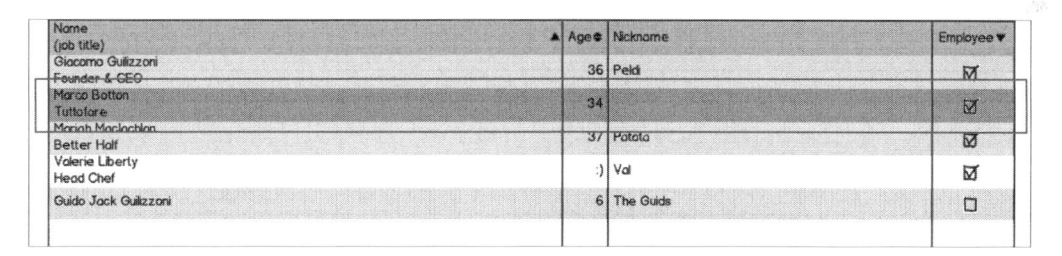

The row you selected is now highlighted. You will notice this functionality in most online forms and now you can depict it directly in your wireframes. It is very useful.

Building Data Tables

Adding a scroll bar

Scroll bars are used to display large amounts of data on a single page. This can come in handy when you want to keep the user's focus on the current page, while still being able to show multiple pages of data.

To add a scroll bar, perform the following steps:

1. Click on the data table to activate the Property Inspector.
2. Click on the **Scrollbar** tool, as shown in the following screenshot:

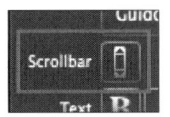

Once clicked, a scroll bar will appear on your data table. While not interactive, this added piece of wireframe functionality helps to set expectations for the viewer as to how this bit of functionality will work in real life. For most wireframes, that's often good enough.

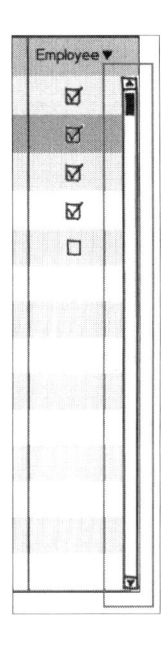

Wireframe project revisited

Now, let's see what you have learned by improving upon your wireframe project and revising the data table to look something like the following figure:

Chapter 4

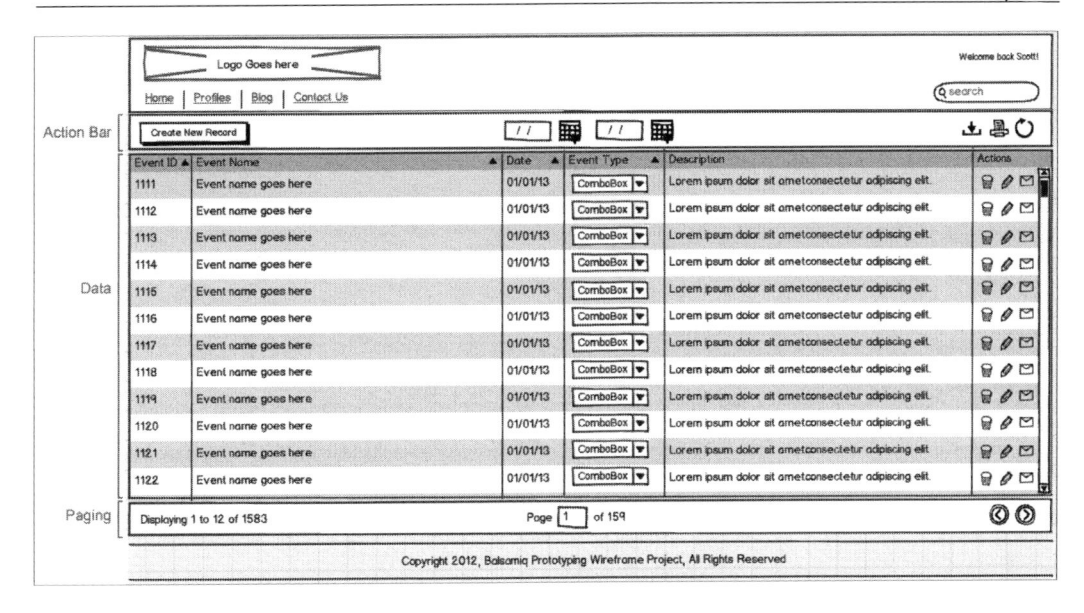

To make understanding and building this data table a bit easier to follow, I have divided it visually into its core sections: Action Bar, Data table, and Paging.

> Keep in mind, what you see above is not completely done using data table formatting, but is the result of some creative Balsamiq trickery, which we will review next.

Revising your project

Let's take a closer look at each section and re-create them in your wireframe project.

Action Bar

The action bar is a control mechanism created for this exercise. It is not mandatory for the data table design, but it is something I often add to data tables as they allow for an element of control over the data and added user functionality. For example, you will notice a button in the Action Bar called **Create New Record**. Upon clicking on it, a popup form might appear allowing you to add data to the table on the fly. Other features include a calendar mechanism for doing a from/to search for data, and some basic tools: download, print, and refresh.

Let's recreate the action bar by performing the following steps:

1. Place a **Rectangle/Canvas/Panel** widget on the canvas.
2. Set **Size:** 1062x44.

Building Data Tables

3. Set **Pos:** `79,97`.
4. Place a **Button** widget.
5. Set **Size:** `128x27`.
6. Set **Pos:** `91,107`.
7. Place two **Date Chooser/Date Picker** widgets.
8. Group them.
9. Set **Pos:** `509,107`.

> For the remaining icons, and for the purpose of this exercise, we are going to skim over a lot of information pertaining to images. But don't worry. Images are an important feature of Balsamiq and will be discussed in detail in the next chapter.

For now, perform the following steps:

1. Place three **Icon** widgets on the canvas roughly in the area where they will sit, as per the previous figure.
2. Double-click on the first **Icon** widget to open the **Icon Library**.
3. Be sure that the icon size slider, located at the bottom of the library window, is set to **S** for small.
4. Double-click on the **Download** icon, as highlighted in the next image, or click on the **Select** button to place it on the canvas, as shown in the following screenshot:

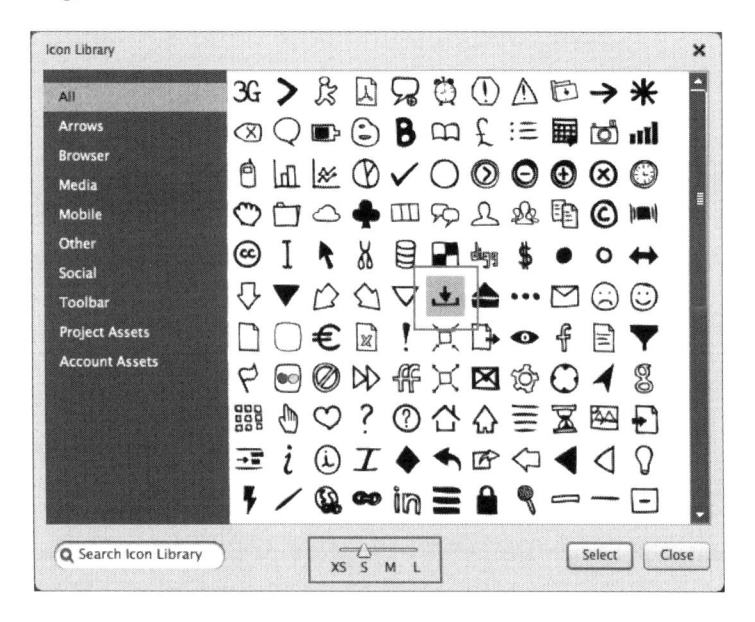

[62]

5. Repeat the steps mentioned earlier for the remaining two icons.

With the three icons in place, select them all and top align them to each other, using the Property Inspector's align tools.

Compare your work to the following sample image:

Data table

Now I want to give you an opportunity to build this next section on your own, as shown in the following screenshot:

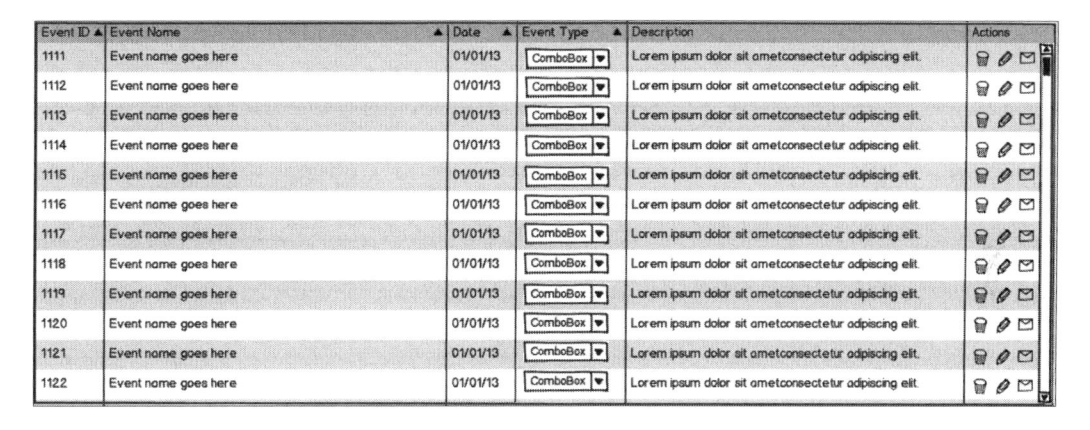

However, if you get stuck, following are a few important things to help guide you:

1. Bring the **Data Table** into edit mode by double-clicking on it.
2. Replace the coordinates in the bottom row with `{5L, 25, 5, 8, 25, 5}`, which will create six columns.
3. Type this text into the top row to create your header: `Event ID, Event Name, Date, Event Type, Description, Actions`.
4. Re-type the text across the second row, as shown in the example above.
5. Leave the fourth column, **Event Type**, empty.

   This space is reserved for the **ComboBox** widget. To make it empty, add a comma in edit mode specifying the fourth column, but leave it blank, as shown in the following screenshot:

Building Data Tables

The sixth column, **Actions**, will also remain empty to make room for the three **Image** widgets that you will place there. There is no need to add a comma to create this column as you already specified its width using the coordinates in the second step.

> By the way, that funny looking text you see in the **Description** column, **Lorem ipsum dolor sit ametconsectetur adipiscing elit**, is referred to as greek or dummy text. It is used in wireframing to show what text will look like without having to type any real content. Rather than trying to retype it, visit `http://www.lipsum.com/` and grab some of your own dummy text.

With the text in the second row complete, copy and paste what you typed to create a total of 12 rows.

Once that is done, perform the following steps:

1. Click outside the table to leave edit mode.
2. Place a **Combo Box** widget into the empty space of the fourth column, **Event Type**.
3. Copy and paste it to fill in the other empty spaces below it and left align them to each other, as shown in the following screenshot:

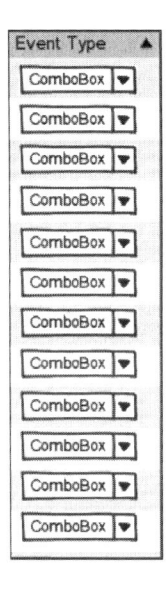

4. Place three **Icon** widgets over the sixth column, **Actions**.
5. Double-click on each to open the **Icon library** and place the images.

6. Set the image size slider to **XS** for extra small.

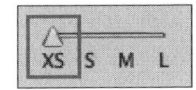

7. Top-align all three images to each other, and group them.
8. Copy and paste the grouped icons to fill in the other empty spaces in the column, and left-align them to each other.

So does your data table match the original image? If so, great! If not, no worries! Just keep at it until it does.

Paging

The final piece of this data table puzzle is the footer, which I call the paging bar. Paging is a way to view multiple pages of data without ever leaving the page, but more on that in a moment.

For now, let's recreate the paging bar by performing the following steps:

1. Place a **Rectangle/Canvas/Panel** widget on the canvas.
2. Set **Size:** 1062x44.
3. Set **Pos:** 79,530.
4. Place a **Label/String of Text** widget and type: Displaying 1 to 12 of 1583.
5. Set **Pos:** 91,540.

To create the middle portion of the paging bar, I used a combination of a **Label/String of Text** widget and a **Rectangle** widget, as shown in the following screenshot:

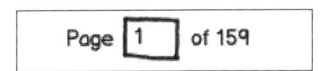

If this were a coded interface, this functionality would give the user the ability to type a page number into the field, press **Enter** and go directly to that page's data.

Here's how to create it in Balsamiq. Perform the following steps:

1. Place a **Label/String of Text** widget in the footer and type: Page of 159. **Leave some space for the rectangle widget, as shown.**
2. Set **Pos:** 533,540.

Building Data Tables

3. Place a **Text Input/Text Field** widget on the canvas.
4. Double-click the widget and type the number 1 inside the text field.
5. Set **Size:** 35x27.
6. Place the **Text Input** widget in the empty space.

Lastly, you will need two **Icon** widgets to create the paging buttons. These buttons would allow the user to click through multiple pages of data while staying on the same page. The only thing changing would be the content in the data table.

To place the paging buttons, perform the following steps:

1. Place two **Icon** widgets on the paging bar.
2. Double-click on one of the widgets to open the **Icon Library**.
3. Locate the button image, otherwise known as **Circle >, Next, Play** and place it on the canvas, as shown in the following screenshot:

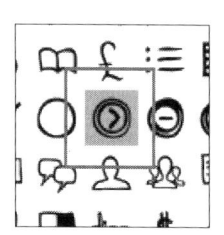

4. With the image selected, click on the **Rotate 90°** tool in the Property Inspector.

    This button will duplicate the image and flip it in the opposite direction. In terms of our design, you now have a back and next button to review page after page of data.

5. Select both buttons and top-align them to each other.
6. Group them.
7. Set **Pos:** 1068,538.

That was a lot of work, but if you followed along then I am sure your finished wireframe looks great. This was truly an exercise to test your ability to be as detailed as possible. Hopefully, you enjoyed the process, because with Balsamiq and wireframing in general, attention to detail is the key to great results.

Even more tips

By now, you should have a great looking data table and wireframe that is slowly, but surely, turning into a nice looking deliverable that you can show to clients, stakeholders, developers, whomever. Later in this book, we will be putting all of these separate pages together to form a clickable, interactive prototype where you can really show off your work.

For now, let's go over a few important tips that are great to know when working with data tables in Balsamiq and as a designer of usable interfaces in general.

Formatting: Readability is usability

It is important to notice how much time and effort we have been spending on formatting. Whether it's text on a page, placing a button, building a web form or creating a data table, formatting is essential for effective usability. Formatting creates consistency and gives your users confidence that what they are seeing is professional and worthy of their time.

Of course, what I am telling you here just scratches the surface. To learn more about formatting, design, and good usability technique in general, read *Chapter 7, Parting Thoughts: Resources and Recommendations*, for some great resources that will point you in the right direction.

Data table details

Here are some additional tips that will take you a long way towards great wireframing and great design in general.

Learn more/see more

Always keep your data at a manageable, readable level. Avoid information overload. Focus on what is most important for the viewer and don't go over that limit. If you need to show them more information, simply offer functionality that allows them to do so. For example, offer a text link or a button that says **Learn More** or **See More**. Perhaps this takes them to a new page, or a popup with additional information. Give users a choice and some control over the content and you will have happy users.

Padding table columns

Here is a key formatting tip that goes a long way: Be sure to add some extra padding to your table columns to avoid the text bumping up against the left and right columns, making it harder to read. Balsamiq automatically does this for you, but you will need to specify this when handing your work to a developer for coding.

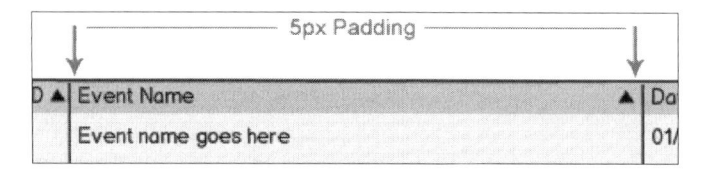

As shown in the previous example, when coding a data table, you simply add 5 pixels of padding to each side of the column.

Aligning text

Generally speaking, it is safe to left-align all of your columns. In fact, the only time you might want to right-align is if the table is displaying decimal-based numbers, like dollar amounts. Doing so allows zeros and the decimal points to align properly. Even so, when doing this, all column headers should remain left-aligned.

Maximum column width

As you design data tables, be sure to know how much data will be in each column. For example, if you are displaying phone numbers, will they be U.S. based or will there be European phone numbers as well? Will zip codes contain just five digits, or more? Will a comments column be added for users to type full paragraphs to text?

A good rule of thumb is to determine the longest piece of data for a given column and adjust that column's width accordingly.

Mac and PC compatibility issues

Lastly, if you are planning to share your Balsamiq wireframes across operating systems, be sure to check your work on both a Mac and PC before doing so. In my experience, I have noticed discrepancies, especially with data tables, when working cross platform. Items can shift, text can misalign and column widths may not look the same.

While this problem may have been fixed as of this writing, be sure to keep it in mind. If you find you are having issues, be sure to reach out to the folks at Balsamiq. They are very receptive to comments and critique and often address issues in a timely fashion.

Summary

In this chapter, you were introduced to data tables, how to format them and what to think about when designing for your project. In addition, you now have some great tips for formatting tables and some overall design tips as well. Best of all, you now have a lot of new tools to work with and can have fun experimenting as well.

In the next chapter, we will work more with images while incorporating a lot of what we have already covered and continue to expand your wireframe project.

Ok. Are you still with me? Great! Let's continue...

5
Icons, Images, and Text

If you are serious about wireframing then, before long, you will be creating some very interesting designs, much of which will contain icons, images, and text. We have already used all three in the previous chapters and now it is time to take a closer look, utilizing what you already know and building upon it.

> As a reminder, all the examples in this chapter, and throughout this book, were created using the latest version of Balsamiq, 2.1.19 at the time of this writing. If you are using an older version, some of the examples presented in this chapter may not work.

The following list shows what we will cover in this chapter:

- Exploring icons
- Importing icons
- Images
- Text usage and formatting
- Additional tips

Exploring icons

One of my favorite things about Balsamiq is its attention to detail, expressed not only through the application's ease of use, but also via the many tools that allow for a clear and concise visual expression of ideas.

Icons, Images, and Text

Let's explore some of them by re-creating the following mockup:

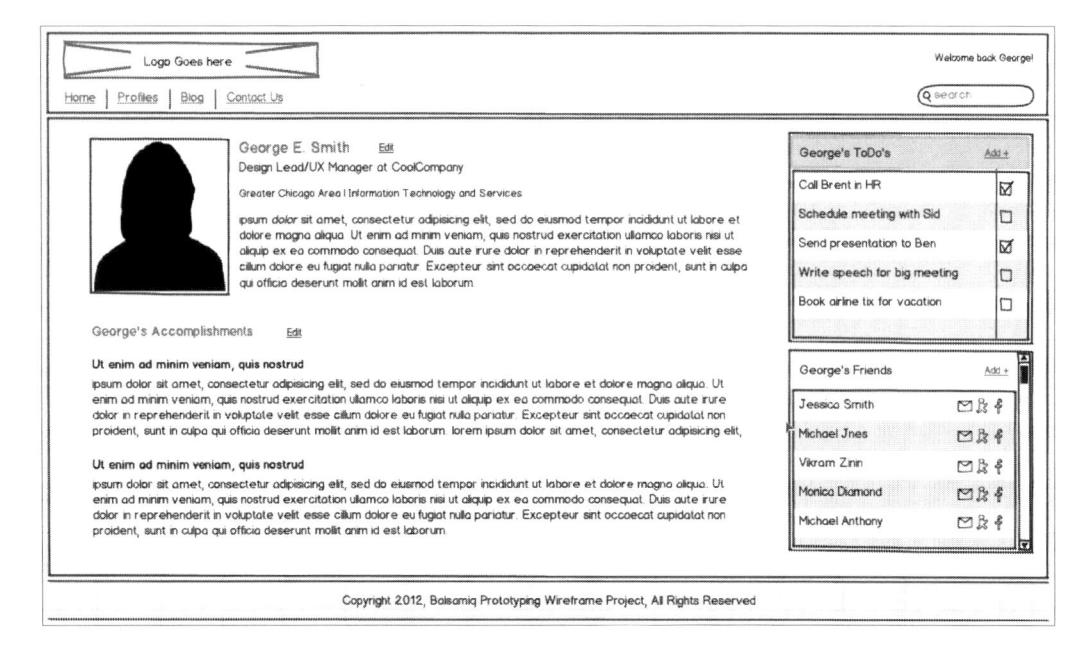

This mockup re-creates a user profile, along with functionality that will allow for interactivity, but we will get into that a little later. For now, let's get started by building this wireframe.

Perform the following steps:

1. Open `project_mockup_2.bmml`.

   We will start with the component called **George's Friends**, located under **George's ToDos** in the right-hand column, as shown in the following screenshot:

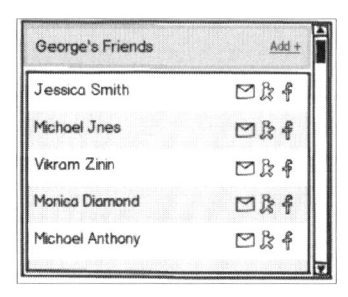

2. Copy and paste the **George's ToDos** component.
3. Set **Pos:** 866,339.

4. Change the title of the new component to **George's Friends**.
5. Bring the data table into edit mode by double-clicking on it.
6. Remove all the items in the second column.

   Removing a column is as easy as deleting any text that follows a comma. Be sure to delete the comma as well.
7. Next, edit the remaining text by typing the names in the example or make up your own. Just be sure to create enough names so that you have five rows.

When you are finished, your component should look something like the following screenshot:

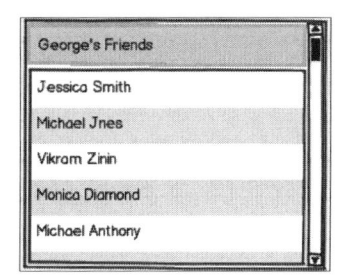

Importing icons

The next step is to add some icons to the component by placing three **Icon** widgets to the right of the name in the first row. Once placed, open the **Icon Library**.

If you recall, in the previous chapter, you can open the **Icon Library** by double-clicking on an **Icon** widget. There is, however, an alternate way to open it via the Property Inspector.

Select one of the **Icon** widgets you just placed and click on the down arrow to the right of the **icon search** text field in the Property Inspector, as shown in the following screenshot:

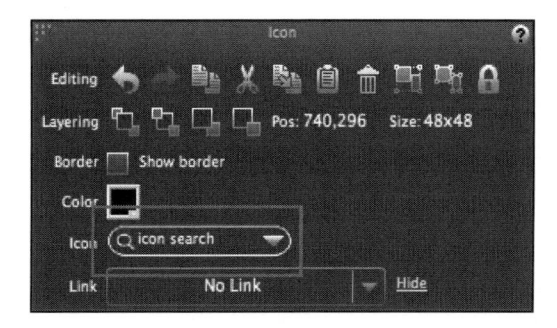

Icons, Images, and Text

Once clicked, the **Icon Library** dialogue window will appear.

The Icon Library

The **Icon Library** is a large collection of Balsamiq provided icons, along with links to sort them on the left-hand side of the window. Use these links to narrow down your search or just select **All** to view every icon available, as shown in the following screenshot:

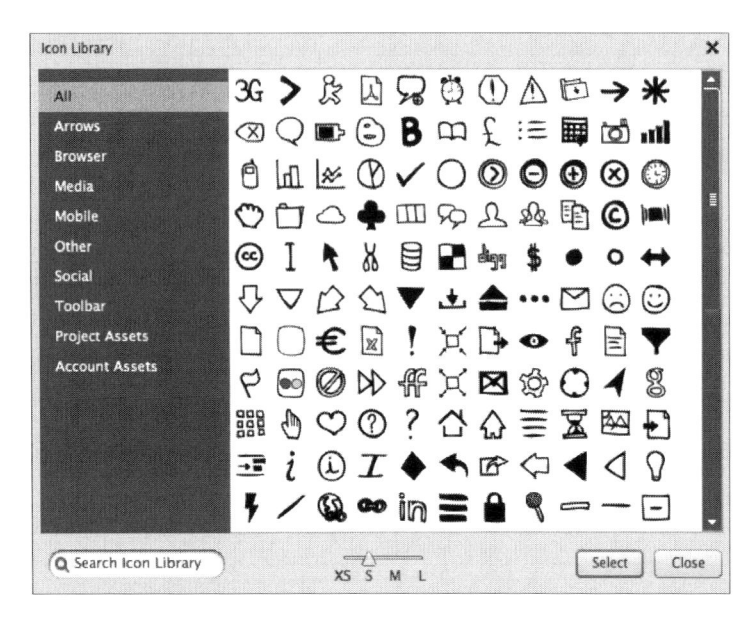

Similar to **Quick Add**, you can also search for icons using the **Search Icon Library** search field located at the lower left of the window and/or the **icon search** text field in the Property Inspector. When you do, notice that both will autocomplete and show a visual representation of what Balsamiq thinks you are searching for. Give it a try.

When you have found what you are looking for; in this example it's the icons for e-mail, instant messaging (IM), and Facebook; place them on the canvas by either double-clicking on each image or by clicking on the **Select** button located at the bottom right of the dialogue window, as shown in the following screenshot:

Be sure that the icon size slider at the bottom of the **Icon Library** window is set to **XS** for extra small, as shown in the following screenshot:

[74]

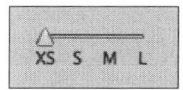

After you have placed all three icons, perform the following steps:

1. Space them evenly using the **Align Middle** and **Top Align** tools in the Property Inspector.
2. Group them.
3. Set **Pos:** 1045,390.
4. Copy and paste the group into the remaining rows.
5. Select them all and left-align them to each other using the **Align Left** tool in the Property Inspector.

Finally, finish the **George's Friends** component as follows:

1. Place a **Label/String of Text** widget in the header bar.
2. Type Add +.
3. Set **Font size:** 10.
4. Set **Pos:** 1071,353.

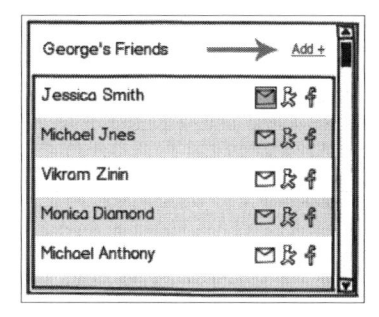

In the real world **Add +** would function as a link control that allows editing of the component. We will put this functionality to work in *Chapter 6, Presenting your Work*.

5. Use the **Underline** tool in the Property Inspector to underline the text, as shown in the following screenshot:

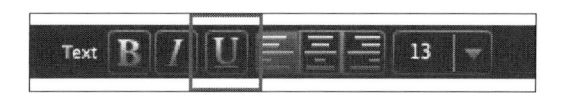

Icons, Images, and Text

6. Change its color to dark blue using the **Color** changer in the Property Inspector, as shown in the following screenshot:

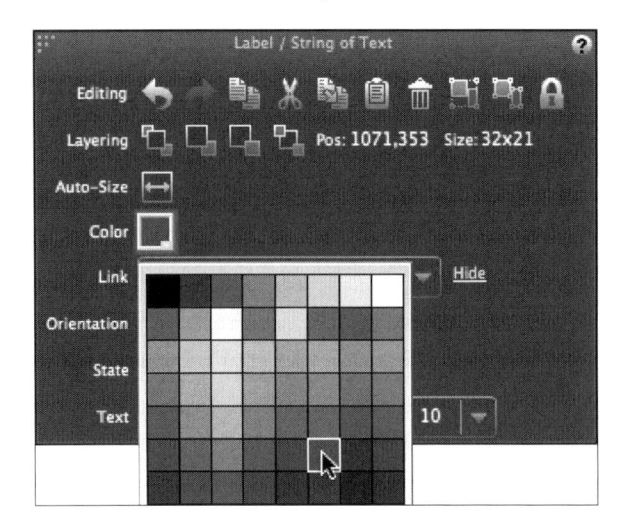

7. Now copy the **Add +** text and place it in the header of **George's ToDos** component above it.
8. Once placed, left align them to each other, as shown in the following screenshot:

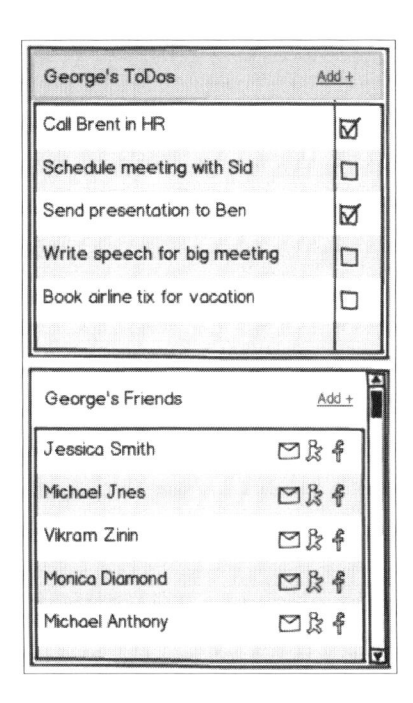

How did you do? Does your work match the example? If not, keep at it. Practice makes perfect, as they say.

Images

It is easy to see how useful and beneficial icons are to your wireframe. Now let's take a closer look at images.

With `project_mockup_2.bmml` still open on your screen, perform the following steps:

1. Place an **Image** widget on the canvas.
2. **Set Pos:** 125,121.
3. **Set Size:** 146x164.
4. Double-click on the widget to open the **Load Image** dialogue window, as shown in the following screenshot:

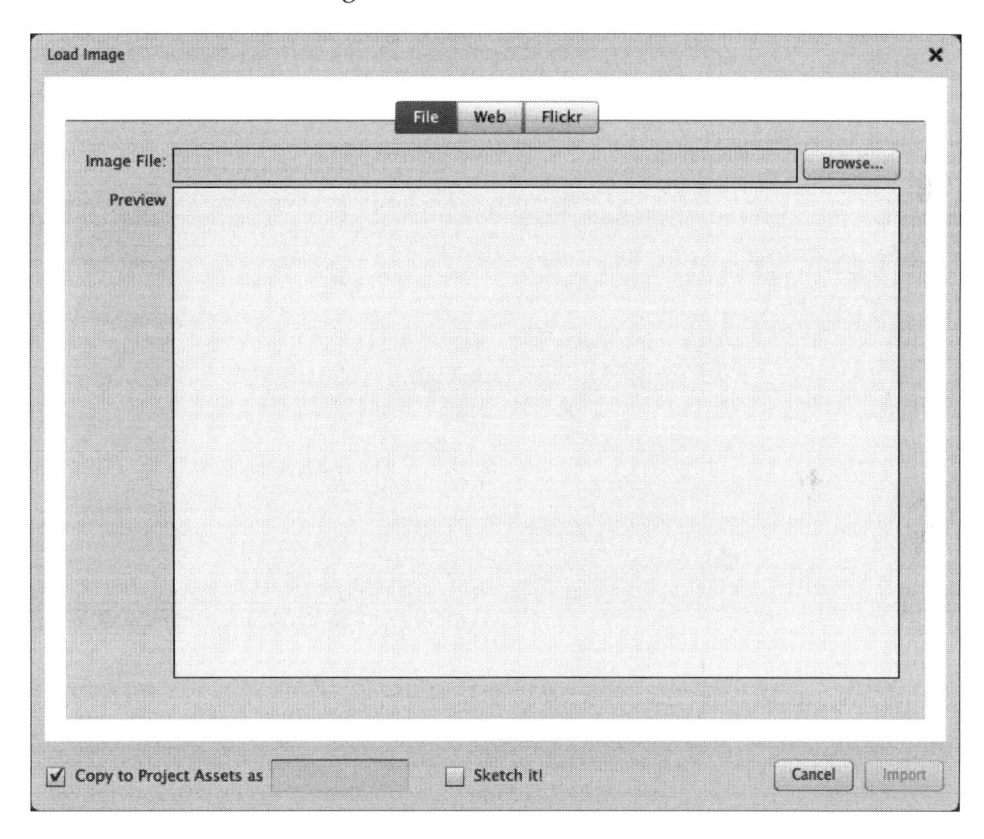

Icons, Images, and Text

The Load Image window

The **Load Image** dialogue window offers three ways to import images: **File**, **Web,** and **Flickr**.

- **File** allows you to import images from your hard drive
- **Web** provides a URL text field to type in the address of an image from an online source
- **Flickr** allows you to type in key words that return related images from the Flickr database of images

For the purposes of our exercise, we will import an image from the images folder that you downloaded earlier.

With the **Load Image** dialogue window open, perform the following steps:

1. Select the **File** tab, if it's not already selected.
2. Click on the **Browse** button, and navigate to the folder: **balsamiq_project_files | assets**.
3. Select `profile_image.png`.
4. Click on the **Import** button.

When the image loads, click on the **Show Border** checkbox in the Property Inspector to give your new image a border, to separate it more clearly from the rest of the page, as shown in the following screenshot:

That's really all there is to it. It's that simple. Now that you know how to import an image file from your computer, try it again using the **Web** and **Flickr** import methods.

> The image you import will fit into the box you create. If you want a large image, then the image box needs to be large as well.

For the record, you can also activate the **Load Image** dialogue window via the Property Inspector.

To do that, perform the following steps:

1. Click on an **Image** on the canvas to expose the Property Inspector.
2. Click on the down arrow in the **Image** drop-down menu.
3. Select **Import Image**, as shown in the following screenshot:

Copying images to project assets

If you recall back in *Chapter 3, Working with Symbols*, we discussed the `assets` folder. This is where Balsamiq stores all of your files, symbols, images, and so on, that are not your wireframe files.

In case you missed it, Balsamiq actually references the `assets` folder within the **Load Image** dialogue window. By clicking on it, you can load images into the `assets` folder automatically.

Perform the following steps:

1. Re-activate the **Load Image** dialogue window by double-clicking on an image on the canvas.
2. With the **File** tab selected, browse for any image on your computer's hard drive.
3. Before you press the **Import** button, click the checkbox in the lower-left corner of the window titled **Copy to Project Assets**, as shown in the following screenshot:

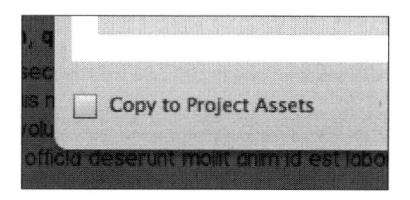

When you check the box, the title of the image will also appear in the text field. You can rename it or leave it as is.

[79]

Icons, Images, and Text

4. Press the **Import** button to place the image on the canvas.

   As you do this, the image is simultaneously saved to your project's `assets` folder.

> If you load an image in the **Load Image** dialogue and find that the **Import** button in the lower right is disabled, it could mean one of two things: Either an image with the same name already exists in the folder, in which case you need to rename the new one, or Balsamiq does not recognize the file extension. For example, Balsamiq does not recognize `.jpeg`. To fix it, change the extension to `.jpg`. Doing either of these will activate the **Import** button.

Image not found

Before moving on, I have one more important piece of information to share with you. Once you place an image onto the canvas from your hard drive, that image must remain in that location. Move it and Balsamiq will have no idea where it went.

Instead, you will see the following screenshot:

This is perhaps the best argument for keeping your wireframe images as an icon collection in the `assets` folder. It is equally compelling if you decide to share your wireframe files with friends and associates.

Cropping images

A new feature in recent versions of Balsamiq is the crop feature. This can be a very handy tool for doing simple editing tasks and, if for nothing else, it keeps you working in the application, rather than having to open an external image-editing application like Photoshop.

The following steps demonstrate how to use it:

1. Select the image you placed earlier on the canvas and click on the **Crop** icon in the Property Inspector, as shown in the following screenshot:

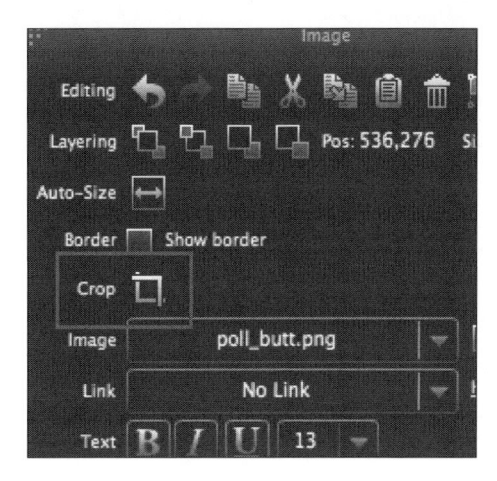

   When clicked, the canvas will go dark except for the area that is cropped. You will also see a series of squares around the crop box. These are resizing handles.

2. Click-and-drag any one of them to resize the crop area, as shown in the following screenshot:

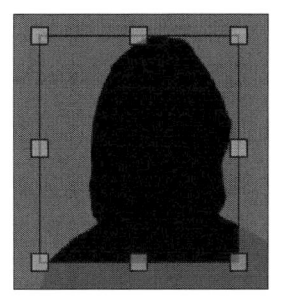

In addition to the grab handles, you will also see a green bar at the top of the canvas with two buttons and a crop size measurement, as shown in the following screenshot:

Icons, Images, and Text

They are used to perform the following functions:

- **Crop Image** is used when you have a satisfactory crop around an image and you are ready to submit the changes. Pressing *Return/Enter* on the keyboard will perform the same action.
- **Cancel** is used when you want to escape out of crop mode with no changes. Pressing the *Esc* key will perform the same action.
- **Cropped size** displays the height and width of the image crop area. The number changes on the fly as you resize the crop area.

Text usage and formatting

Working with text in Balsamiq can take some time getting used to. While Balsamiq does offer a fair amount of text control and some familiar formatting tools, it is not a word processor. As a result, there are some formatting tips specific to Balsamiq that you should become familiar with.

Let's get started by performing the following steps:

1. Open `project_mockup_2.bmml`.
2. Click on the name, **George E. Smith**, next to the profile image.
3. Press *Enter/Return* on your keyboard or double-click on the text widget to activate it.

   This will turn the textbox into an editable area, as shown in the following screenshot:

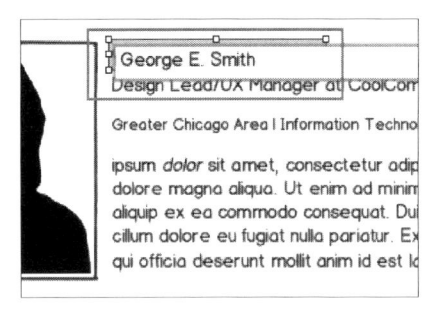

4. Type a name into the text field or leave it as is.
5. Click anywhere outside the textbox to deactivate it.

   You can also press the *Esc* key to perform the same action.

6. Using the Property Inspector's **Text** formatting tools, apply the following to George's name:
    - **Bold**
    - **Align Left**
    - **Font size**: 16

Feel free to change the color of the text too, using the color selector in the Property Inspector.

Additional text tools

Formatting with the Property Inspector is obviously useful. But what if you wanted even greater control over the text in your wireframe? What if you wanted to not only format sentences and paragraphs, but also format specific words within them? With Balsamiq, that is easy to do.

Double-click on the paragraph of text in `project_mockups_2.bmml` and notice the formatting elements surrounding the following highlighted text:

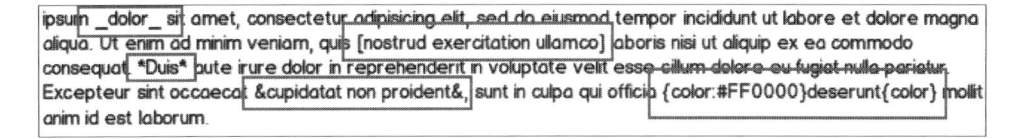

Let's take a closer look at what's going on:

- Italicized: Place an underscore before and after a word or sentence
- Hyperlink: Place brackets before and after a word or sentence
- Bold: Place an asterisk before and after a word or sentence
- Disabled text: Place a dash before and after a word or sentence
- Underline: Place an ampersand before and after a word or sentence
- Color: Add color to the text, as shown in the previous screenshot

Icons, Images, and Text

Combining formatting styles

Once you have all the formatting tricks, as mentioned previously, under your belt, you can combine them to make hybrid styles. For example, maybe you want to make a word bold and underline it as well.

Let's try this by performing the following steps:

1. Place a **Label/String of Text** widget on the canvas and type the following:
   `*Bold* an &Underlined& word by *&doing this&*.`

   Be sure to copy all the formatting symbols and text as shown.

2. Once typed, deselect the widget and watch it turn into the following:

   Bold an <u>Underlined</u> word by **<u>doing this</u>**

Try formatting more of the text throughout your wireframe and see what you can come up with by using these formatting tricks.

Single line text versus paragraph

When adding text to a wireframe, you have choices. Whether you are writing a single sentence or a full paragraph, in Balsamiq you have the option to do both using the **Label/String of Text** widget or the **Paragraph of Text** widget.

Label/String of Text allows you to type a single line of text, as displayed in the following screenshot:

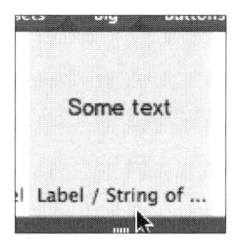

Some text
Label / String of ...

Paragraph of Text is an aptly named widget as it allows you to type multiple lines of text, as displayed in the following screenshot:

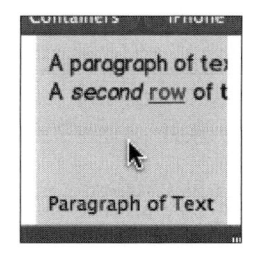

Let's take a moment now to add some additional text to your wireframe.

[*Although **Paragraph of Text** can be used to write a single line of text, try to use the right widget for the job. You will find it to your benefit as your project grows. You are just going to have to trust me on that one.*]

When we are done, your canvas should look like the following screenshot:

Once again, I am going to leave it to you to do most of the work. The following are some tips to think about as you complete this exercise:

1. Don't retype.

    Copy and paste the paragraph already on the page and create the two additional paragraphs, as shown in the previous screenshot.

Icons, Images, and Text

2. Using the **Label/String of Text** widget, re-create the title **George's Accomplishments** and the headlines beneath it, as shown in the following screenshot:

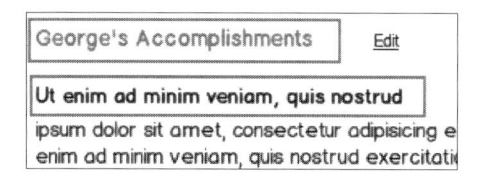

3. Change the font size of **George's Accomplishments** to 14 and make the text **Bold**.
4. Choose a color for the text. Any color will do.

After doing so, perform the following steps:

1. Add another **Label/String of Text** widget and type Edit.
2. Set **Text Size** to 10 and **Underline** it.
3. Set **Pos:** 332,314.
4. Select it all, as shown in the following screenshot:

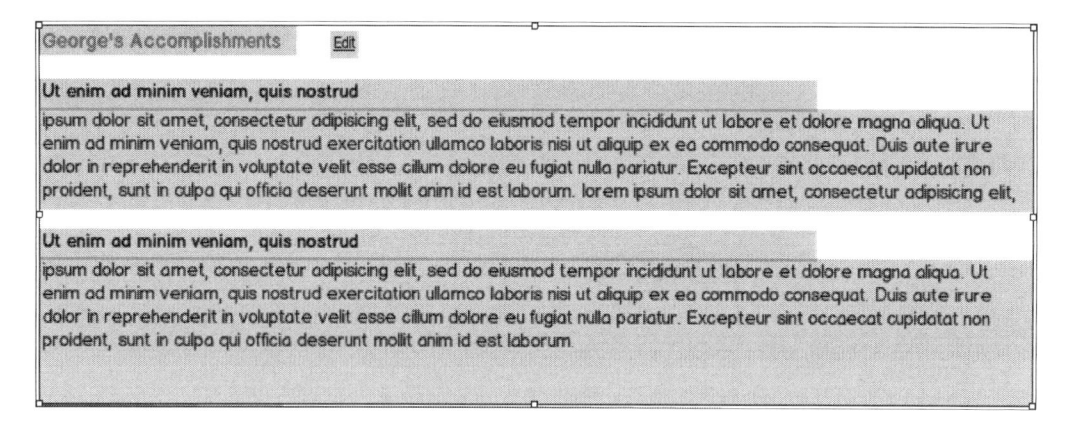

5. Set **Pos:** 125,310.

How did you do? Does your wireframe look like the example? If it does, great work!

Additional tips

Here are some additional tips that I am sure you will find useful and that will aid in your design productivity.

Lorem ipsum

Much of the text you have seen in the examples throughout this book have been what is known as lorem ipsum text, commonly referred to in the design world as dummy text. Dummy text is used to create text for wireframes without having to type or use actual text that can distract from the design itself.

To find dummy text, you can go online to `http://www.lipsum.com/` or you can stay within Balsamiq and use this very cool trick as follows:

1. Open `project_mockup_2.bmml`.
2. Click on the first paragraph under **George's Accomplishments** and double-click, or press **Enter**, to make the content editable.
3. Place the cursor somewhere in the paragraph and type the word `lorem`.

Like magic, Balsamiq provides you with an entire paragraph of lorem ipsum text. Very cool indeed.

Sketch it!

Just as we use dummy text so as to not distract the viewer from our design, Balsamiq offers a way to do this with images as well, using a feature called **Sketch it!**.

To use it, perform the following steps:

1. Double-click the image in `project_mockup_2.bmml` to open the **Load Image** dialogue window.

   At the bottom of the window you will notice the **Sketch it!** checkbox.

2. Click the checkbox to check it/sketch it and press **Import**, as shown in the following screenshot:

Icons, Images, and Text

Here is a before and after image I created using **Sketch it!**. I'll let you decide which one looks better. As you can see, the image on the right looks more in line with the black and white style of your wireframe, thus, lessening the potential for distractions as you present your design ideas.

Auto-Size

Auto-Size is a Property Inspector tool that will return an image to its original size, as shown in the following screenshot:

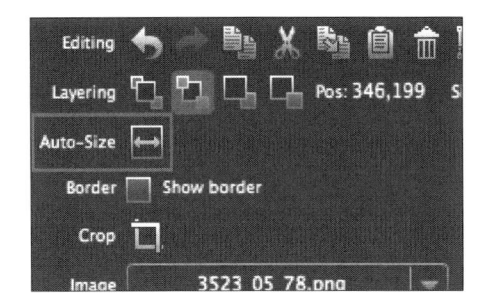

To use it, simply select an image that you want to return to its original dimensions and click the **Auto-Size** icon. Like almost everything else in Balsamiq, it is really that easy.

Summary

Whew! That was a lot to cover in one chapter. But, as you know by now, icons, images, and text are the key ingredients in your wireframe soup. Having completed the chapter, you are now equipped with the most important information about how to use these tools effectively. We are almost at the end, but we are not quite finished yet. In the next chapter, we are going to put it all together and turn your wireframe into a clickable prototype and ready it for presentation.

Let's get to it!

6
Presenting Your Work

You've followed the exercises in this book. You've put together a nice set of wireframes that demonstrate your skills in Balsamiq. Now what? How are you going to present it? How does it all come together? Will your project become a clickable prototype? PDF? PNG image? Raw XML? All of the above? No worries! In this chapter all of these questions will be answered.

The following list shows what we will cover:

- Prototyping
- Linking pages
- Additional interactivity
- Notes and documentation (also known as markup)
- Exporting for presentation
- XML in Balsamiq

Prototyping

Prototyping is the method for testing your ideas, user flows, navigation, design, and overall usability for the product that you have created. Prototyping also allows end users to interact with your designs and to provide valuable feedback before anything is ever coded. It is also an opportunity to present your work to stakeholders and/or clients before spending long hours skinning your design in Photoshop or finding that you may have missed a few important details along the way, requiring some extensive rework as a result.

As you can see, prototyping is a valuable communication tool. To give you a better idea of just how effective it can be, let's turn your wireframe project into one.

Presenting Your Work

Symbols revisited

We will begin by opening all of your project files in Balsamiq. If you have been using the files provided with this book, they will be in your **balsamiq_project_files** folder, as shown in the following screenshot:

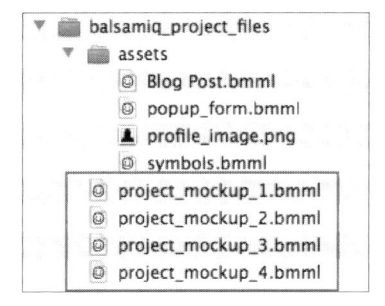

With the files open, check that all the page headers are symbols. You will recall that symbols turn green when clicked and produce a green override bar when double-clicked, as shown in the following screenshot:

Now that you have confirmed that the headers are indeed symbols, let's link the navigation in the header to their respective pages.

Wait. There's something wrong!

The navigation text doesn't match the pages we created. I realized this error as I was writing this chapter and decided to keep it in to demonstrate how easily mistakes can be missed so close to the end of a project. The good news is we planned ahead so this error can be easily fixed.

Perform the following steps:

1. Open `project_mockup_1.bmml`.
2. Double-click on the header.

3. Click on **Edit** in the green symbol override bar to go to the header **Symbol Library** master page.
4. Double-click on the **Link Bar, Navigation** widget to make it editable.
5. Change the navigation to: **Home, Profile, Blog, Data**, as shown in the following screenshot:

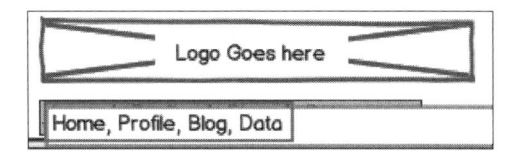

6. Save your work.
7. Close the **Symbol Library** page.

Since we made the changes via the **Symbol Library** master page, the navigation was updated on every page in your project. Check to make sure.

Linking pages

Now we are ready to link the navigation to their respective pages. With the navigation selected, you will see a section in the Property Inspector called **Links**. You will notice that the links you just updated are represented there as well, as shown in the following screenshot:

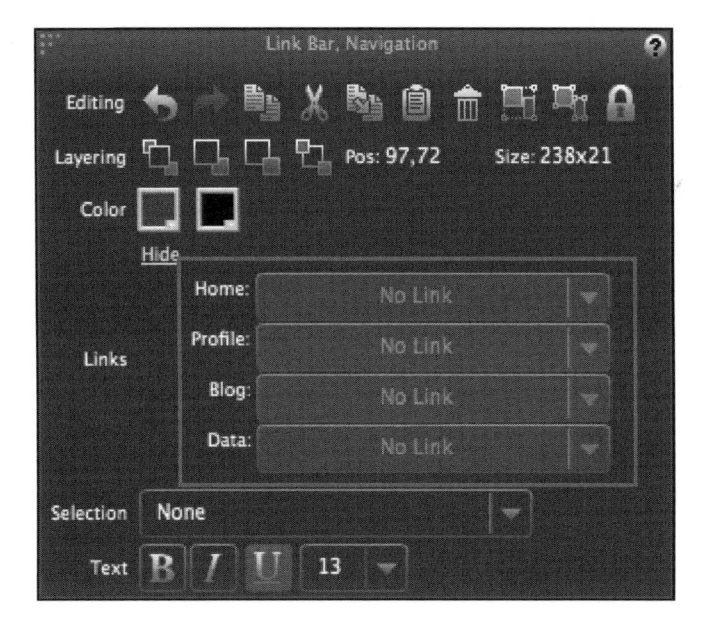

Presenting Your Work

To link the pages, perform the following steps:

1. In the Property Inspector, press the **Home** menu down arrow.
2. In the drop-down menu that appears, select **project_mockup_1**.
3. Do the same for each subsequent page, until they link to their correct pages.

   Profile: **project_mockup_2**, Blog: **project_mockup_3**, Data: **project_mockup_4**.

When finished, your navigation should look like the following screenshot:

Notice the red arrows that appear next to each link. This is Balsamiq's way of indicating that these areas are now linked.

Presentation mode

You may be wondering why the links don't actually work when you click on them. That's because you first have to be in the presentation mode. Presentation mode is what Balsamiq uses to present your work to the outside world.

To activate it, click the icon, known as the **Full Screen Presentation** button, in the upper-right corner of your Balsamiq application window, as shown in the following screenshot:

You can also press *Command + F/Ctrl + F* on your keyboard to activate it. Once in the presentation mode, click the navigation links again. They are now clickable and should link to the pages you specified.

Link types

Presentation mode offers two ways to present links to your audience: Invisible links and visible links.

- Invisible links: In this mode, all link hotspots are transparent, meaning the page will look normal, with no indication that there are any links present. You simply hover your mouse over an area that you know is linked and the cursor will change to a pointing hand, as shown in the following screenshot:

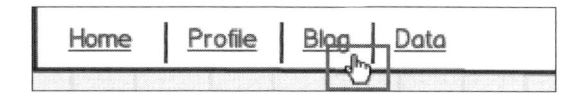

- Visible links: In this mode, all links are visible via shaded blocks around the text. There is also an unmistakable giant blue arrow pointing them out, as shown in the following screenshot:

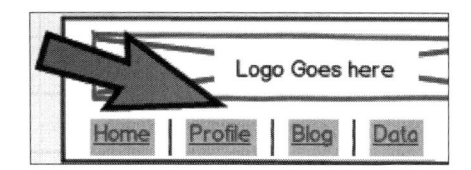

Once you hover over a link, the arrow becomes a giant blue hand pointer. Underneath it, you will also see the page that it is linked to, as shown in the following screenshot:

Keep in mind you can also toggle between the two presentation modes.

Perform the following steps:

1. Hover the mouse pointer over the bottom-right corner of the canvas until you see a set of three icons.
2. Click the first icon, **Show Linking Hints and Cursor**, to toggle between visible and invisible attributes.

    You can also perform this action by using the *L* key on your keyboard.

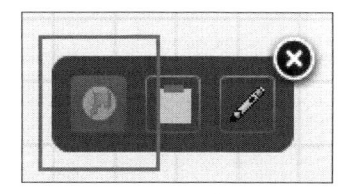

The other two icons

Let's briefly review the remaining two icons in this set as well.

From left to right, they are as follows:

- **Show Markup**: This clipboard icon toggles markup between on and off. Pressing the *K* key will perform the same action. We will cover markup later in this chapter.
- **Edit this mockup**: This pencil icon closes the presentation mode and returns to the wireframe for additional editing. Pressing the *E* key or pressing *Esc* will perform the same action.

Additional interactivity

Now let's add some additional interactivity to your wireframes.

Perform the following steps:

1. Right-click on the page tab for **project_mockup_2** in the file browser, as shown in the following screenshot:

2. In the menu that appears, select **Clone As New Mockup** to make an identical copy of this page, as shown in the following screenshot:

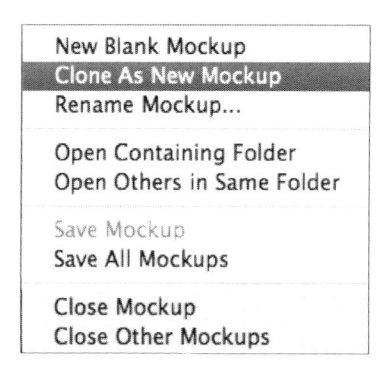

A new page is created called **New Mockup** and is identical to `project_mockup_2.bmml`. Press *Command + S/Ctrl + S* to save it. Name it `project_mockup_2b.bmml`.

Make sure to save this new file in the same folder as the rest of your project files. If you have been using the files provided with this book, then you would place it in the **balsamiq_project_files** folder, as shown in the following screenshot:

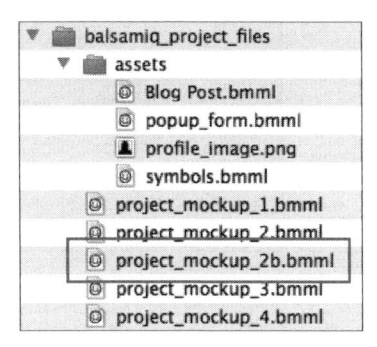

Interactive checkbox

Now let's take it up a notch and create some additional interactivity.

Perform the following steps:

1. Make `project_mockup_2b.bmml` the active page.
2. Double-click on the text in **George's ToDos** to make it editable.

   If the component is grouped, please ungroup it.
3. In the second row, next to **Schedule meeting with Sid**, type an x into the empty brackets, as shown in the following screenshot:

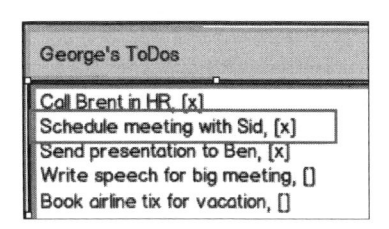

4. Save your work.
5. Return to `project_mockup_2.bmml` and place a **Rectangle/Canvas/Panel** widget on the canvas.
6. Set **Size:** `15x17`.
7. Set **Pos:** `223,80`.

Presenting Your Work

The widget should now look like the following screenshot:

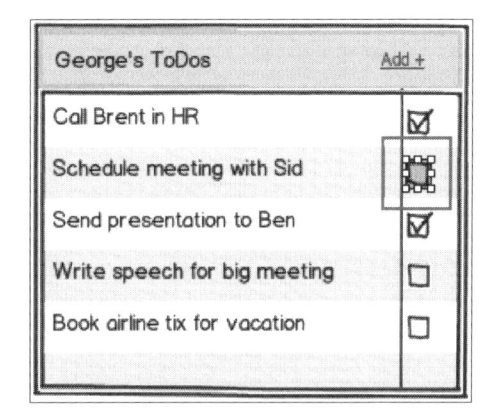

With this new widget selected, perform the following steps:

1. In the Property Inspector, slide the **Opacity** slider all the way to the left.
2. In the **Border Style** section, click on the first icon to remove the border, as shown in the following screenshot:

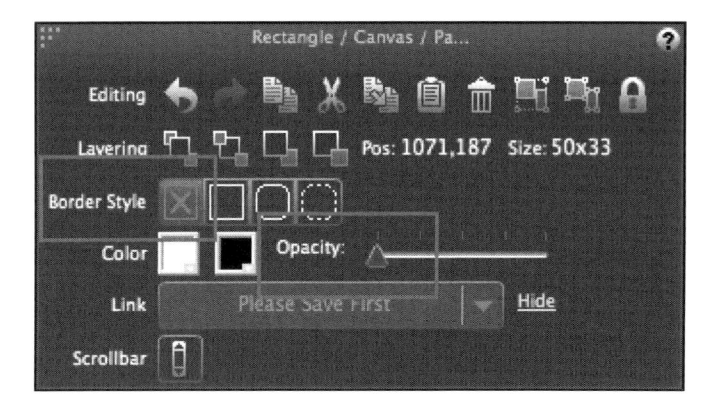

You should now have a totally transparent widget over the checkbox.

> Opacity controls the transparency of an image or widget. For example, to the left of the slider is 0 percent, or totally invisible. To the right of the slider is 100 percent, or fully visible. Each notch in between increases or decreases the transparency.

We will now create some more Balsamiq prototype magic.

Perform the following steps:

1. With the transparent widget still selected, press the **Link** menu in the Property Inspector.
2. Select **project_mockup_2b** from the drop-down list, as shown in the following screenshot:

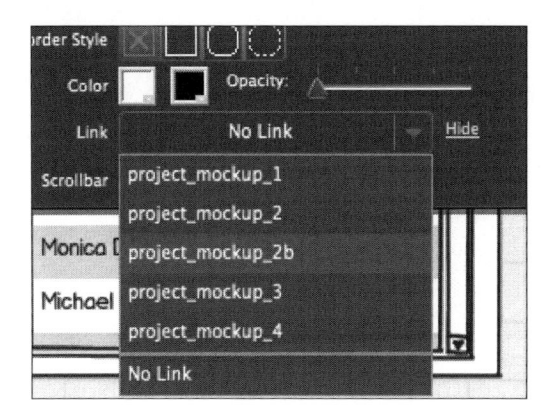

3. Save your work.

A red arrow should now appear within the transparent box. This is to let you know that it has been linked to this new page. With **project_mockup_2** selected, go into the presentation mode and click your newly linked checkbox.

If you did this correctly, it will appear as if you clicked on the page and a check was automatically inserted into the checkbox. You and I know that you went to a new page, but the person viewing it will just see an interactive prototype. Nice work!

Even more interactivity

In this exercise, we are going to add a brand new row of text to **George's ToDos**, via an interactive form.

In the scheme of our design, we are going to use the **Add +** text in **George's ToDos** to launch a form popup dialogue box that allows users to add a new row of text to the component. Of course, to do this, we need to create a new page with the form, and another to show the added row of text. Let's do this now.

Presenting Your Work

Perform the following steps:

1. Open `project_mockup_2.bmml`.
2. Right-click on the page tab and select **Clone as New Mockup**.
   Repeat this step to create a total of two new pages.
3. Name the new files as: `project_mockup_2c.bmml` and `project_mockup_2d.bmml`.
4. As always, save these to your project folder.
5. Open `popup_form.bmml`, which resides in your project's `assets` folder.
6. Select the grouped form and copy/paste it into `project_mockup_2c.bmml`.
7. Set **Pos:** `304,142`.
   Be sure it sits at the very top layer on the page.
8. Ungroup the form, and link the **Save** button to `project_mockup_2d.bmml`.

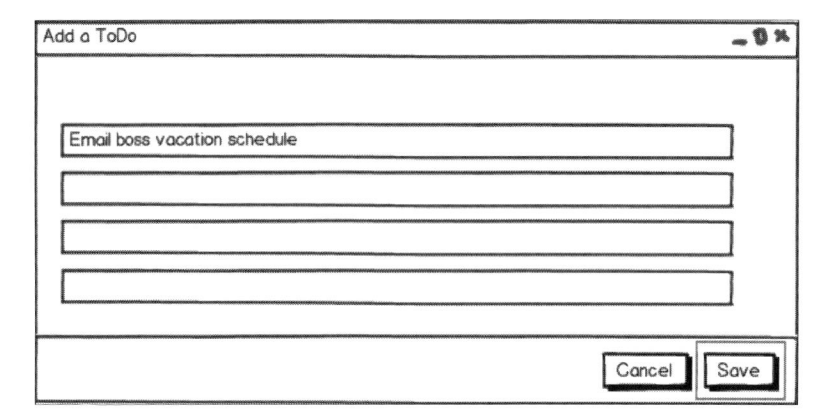

9. Save your changes.
10. Open `project_mockup_2d.bmml`.
11. In **George's ToDos**, make the data table editable.
12. In the bottom row, type: `Email boss vacation schedule, [ ]`.
    Be sure to include the empty brackets.
    Your list should now look like the following screenshot, with the new row added at the bottom:

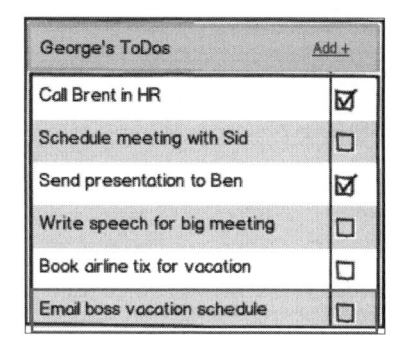

If you notice, back in `project_mockup_2c.bmml`, the form has been pre-filled with this same text in the form text field. The idea is to show that whatever the user types into the form will be added to **George's ToDos**.

13. Return to `project_mockup_2.bmml` and select **Add +** in **George's ToDos**, as shown in the following screenshot:

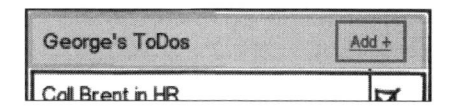

14. Using the Property Inspector, link the text to `project_mockup_2c.bmml`.
15. Go into the presentation mode.
16. Click on **Add +**.
17. When the form appears, click on the **Save** button.

When you click on **Save**, the last row of **George's ToDos** adds a new row containing the text from the form. Sure, you used two separate pages to make this work, but again, to the viewer you added a line of text directly from the form. Remember, with prototyping, how you get to the desired result behind the scenes is secondary to the results themselves.

Now that you know how to create some interactivity, have some fun with it. See where else you can add interactivity and creativity. For example, return to `project_mockup_2.bmml` and add some interactivity to the **Edit** link in the body copy, next to **George's Accomplishments**, as shown in the following screenshot:

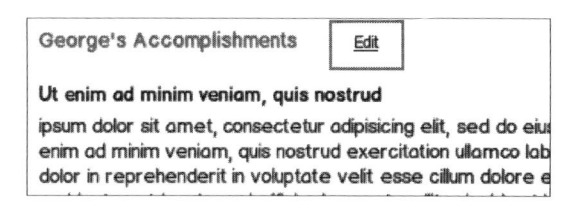

Presenting Your Work

Perhaps clicking on this link changes the page to display an interactive form for editing the text. Maybe it looks something like the following screenshot:

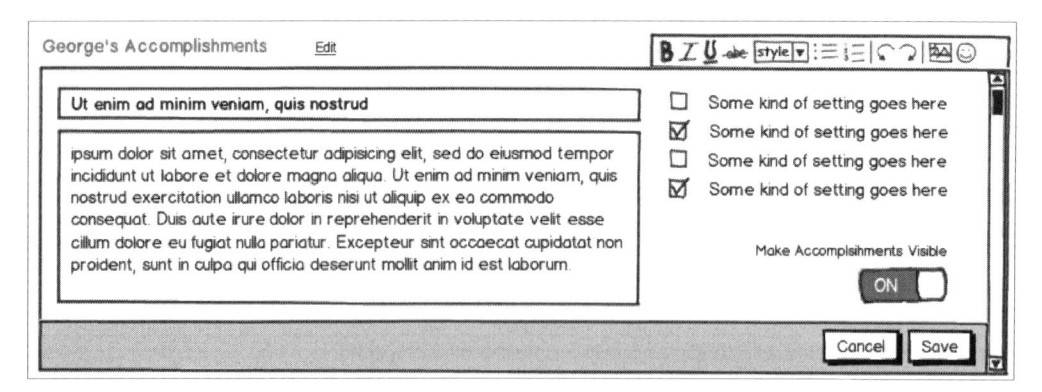

The best part is that with Balsamiq it is totally up to you and your creativity. Explore! See what you can dream up.

> If you want to take a closer look at the wireframe above or the completed versions of any wireframe used in this book, you can do so by going to http://www.packtpub.com and downloading the project files from the **Downloads** section of the book.

Notes and documentation (also known as markup)

Now that we've linked pages and added additional interactivity to your project, let's talk about another important aspect of presenting your work, one that centers on handing your work off to the folks who will code it.

As a wireframe architect, you will often be working closely with developers who are tasked with turning your wireframes into online interfaces, using real code. Their understanding of what you want is key, not only to ensure proper functionality, but also to ensure that your vision, your standards and the user experience matches what you get back from them.

You see, working with developers can often result in a coded interface that looks something like what you had in mind, but is more often closer to an interpretation of your wireframe. In other words, some code may not render properly on screen, alignment may be a bit off due to browser incompatibility and/or some of the details you specified may have been left out due to time and/or budgetary constraints.

The reality is, you really never know what will happen once it is out of your hands. To counter common issues like this requires that you communicate with your development team early and often. It also means preparing your wireframes with enough detail and guidance so that nothing is left to chance or left to interpretation. In other words, you must not only show your work, you must tell its story as well.

Not surprisingly, Balsamiq provides tools to do that as well.

Markup widgets

As you already know, Balsamiq is loaded with useful widgets. Some of these fall under a category called markup. Markup is merely a fancy term for making notes on the page for others to follow. Markup widgets can be found by clicking on the **Markup** button, atop the UI Library, as shown in the following screenshot:

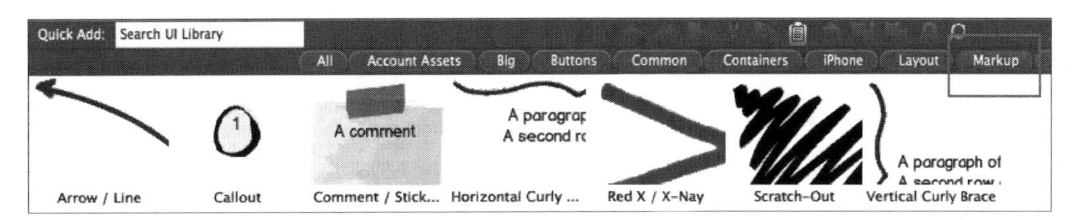

Here, you will find everything you need to document and notate your wireframe, make comments, and essentially make it easy for those viewing your work to follow along.

Once again, I have taken the liberty of adding some markup to your wireframe to give you an idea of what it might look like in the real world.

To view it, perform the following steps:

1. Open `project_mockup_2.bmml`.
2. Click on **Show Markup**.

    That's the button in the upper-right corner of the screen, next to the **Full Screen Presentation** button we used earlier, as shown in the following screenshot:

Feel free to edit what I have done or add some of your own markup. The **Markup** widgets are easy to use as well. Just double-click on them to edit the text. You can also use the Property Inspector to modify and format the mockup widgets. Explore!

Presenting Your Work

Once again, the goal of markup is to be as clear as possible when you hand your work off to other people. It is not the only solution to avoiding issues completely, but markup will at least provide some detail, inspire questions, and engage constructive feedback, which in the end will save you time in the near term and help you to avoid many unnecessary surprises later.

> You can also turn markup on and off by pressing *Command + K/Ctrl + K* on your keyboard. If you are in the presentation mode, you can turn markup on and off simply by pressing *K* on your keyboard.

Exporting for Presentation

Ok! We have seen how to present our work in Balsamiq, but what if we want to share our work outside of the application? Well, I am sure you already know what I am going to say. With Balsamiq, that's easy to do!

Using Balsamiq's exporting functionality, we can share our work as a PDF, a PNG, or even as raw XML code.

Let's review each method.

Exporting to PDF

Exporting your wireframes to PDF allows you to take your work offline and present it in a printable form. In addition, you can also share a PDF online as a downloadable document. The best part is, if your wireframe contains links then your PDF will too! Now that's useful and impressive! Let's export your entire project as a PDF document.

To do this, you must first open all of your project files and make sure the pages are opened in the correct order, that is, **project_mockups_1**, **project_mockups_2**, **project_mockups_2b**, **project_mockups_2c**, **project_mockups_2d**, **project_mockups_3**, **project_mockups_4**.

As a reminder, Balsamiq does not know the order of your pages. When you export to PDF, the order of the pages in your PDF will be in the same order as they are in the file browser. Take a moment to ensure that your pages are in the correct order, as shown in the following screenshot:

| project_mockup_1 | project_mockup_2 | project_mockup_2b | project_mockup_2c | project_mockup_2d | project_mockup_3 | project_mockup_4 |

If not, rearrange them by clicking-and-dragging the tabs in the file browser until they are.

With the pages arranged, perform the following steps:

1. Choose **File | Export all Mockups to PDF**.
2. Keep the default settings in the **PDF Export Options** dialogue box that appears, as shown in the following screenshot:

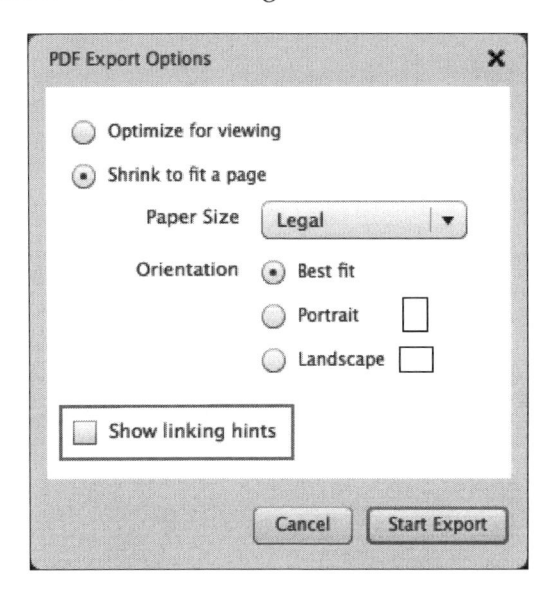

Since exporting to PDF retains all of your links, the export popup offers an optional way to view them. By clicking in the checkbox called **Show linking hints**, your PDF will display visible links, so you and your users will know where to click.

3. Click on the **Start Export** button.
4. Choose where you want to save the PDF.

Once saved, open the PDF to make sure all your pages look correct and are in the correct order. Click on the links to make sure they work too!

> We just exported an entire project to a PDF file, but you can also export a single page or specific pages to PDF as well. To do this, simply open those pages that you want to include and then export them using the same steps as mentioned previously.

Presenting Your Work

Exporting to PNG

Another way to get your wireframes out of Balsamiq is as a PNG image file. As with PDFs, you can export to PNG as a single page or you can export the entire contents of your project folder.

Exporting a single page to PNG

Exporting a single page to PNG is perhaps the most common use of this functionality.

To use it, perform the following steps:

1. Select the page you want to export.
2. Select **File** | **Export to PNG Image**.

You will see where the PNG file went via the small black box that appears in the lower-right corner of your screen. If you find it hard to follow the path specified, you can simply double-click on the box and it will open the folder where the file was placed.

> Your mockup was exported to /Users/sfaranello/Desktop/Packt_Book/thebook/Edits/basamiq_project_files/project_mockup_2c.png. Click here to view.

Exporting individual elements to PNG

In addition to exporting full pages as PNG, you can choose to export individual elements on the page as well.

Perform the following steps:

1. Select a few individual elements on a page.
2. Select **File** | **Export to PNG Image**.

3. Choose **Export Selected** in the dialogue box that appears, as shown in the following screenshot:

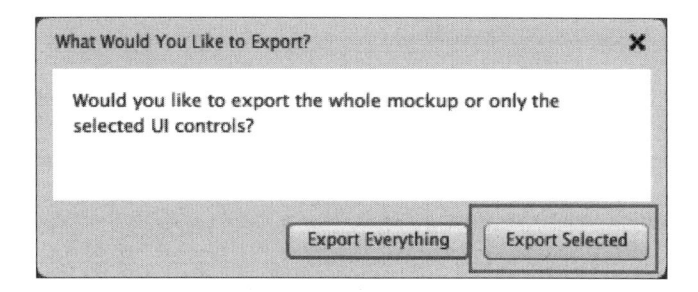

The subsequent PNG image will contain only the elements you selected. Open the one you just created and you will see what I mean.

Exporting an entire project to PNG

Unlike exporting to PDF, which saves all of your open pages as a single, multi-page document, exporting an entire project to PNG will save all of your pages as individual PNG files.

If they are not open already, open all of your wireframe files, once again, and select **File | Export All Mockups to PNG**. You will find that you now have multiple PNG files saved for each of your wireframe pages.

Exporting an image to the clipboard

Exporting an image to the clipboard works very much the same as exporting to PNG, with some differences.

Firstly, instead of saving a PNG file to your hard drive, **File | Export Image to Clipboard** saves the widget to the clipboard. From there, it can be pasted from the clipboard in one of two ways:

- As an image pasted into MS Word, onto your desktop, or into any other application that accepts images
- Directly into Balsamiq

Presenting Your Work

When using the second option, pasting into Balsamiq will activate a popup dialogue box that asks you to name the file, as shown in the following screenshot:

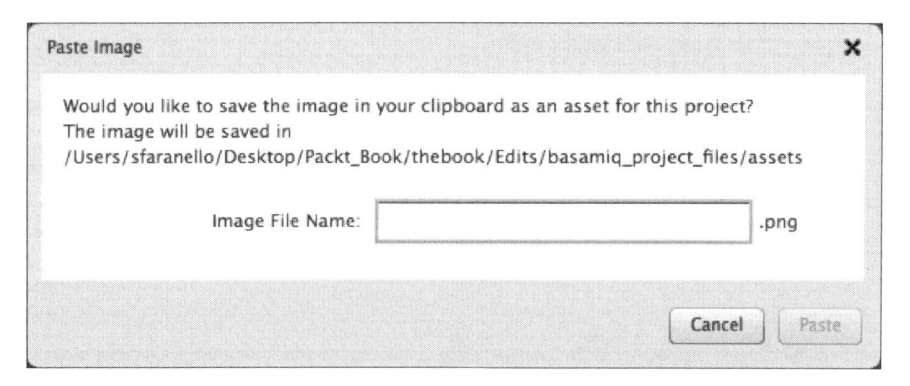

When you click the **Paste** button, the image is automatically saved to your `assets` folder.

> Unlike other methods for exporting, **Export Image to Clipboard** does not allow you to export parts of a page. It's all or nothing.

Lastly, keep in mind that as you work in Balsamiq, you cannot simply copy items to your clipboard using *Command + C/Ctrl + C*, like you would in most other applications. Balsamiq actually reserves *Command + C/Ctrl + C* for another very special use. As a matter of fact, this is a great segue into the next section.

XML in Balsamiq

Balsamiq is a very unique application and we have seen many aspects of that throughout this book. Now, I want to bring to your attention yet another unique feature that turns mild mannered wireframes into raw XML code in an instant.

For the record, I am not a developer and this is not a development book. Nevertheless, for those who are, I am sure you will find this functionality quite useful.

Exporting wireframes as XML

Exporting XML allows you to share raw XML code via e-mail, as imported code into applications that play nice with Balsamiq, like Napkee, http://www.napkee.com—more on that in the next chapter—or you can export it back into Balsamiq to create new pages or widgets.

To use the export feature, simply select **File | Export Mockup XML**. As with exporting to PNG, you can select an entire page or just portions of the page. In addition, once exported you may also see various dialogue boxes, based on what you are attempting to export.

For example, refer to the following screenshot:

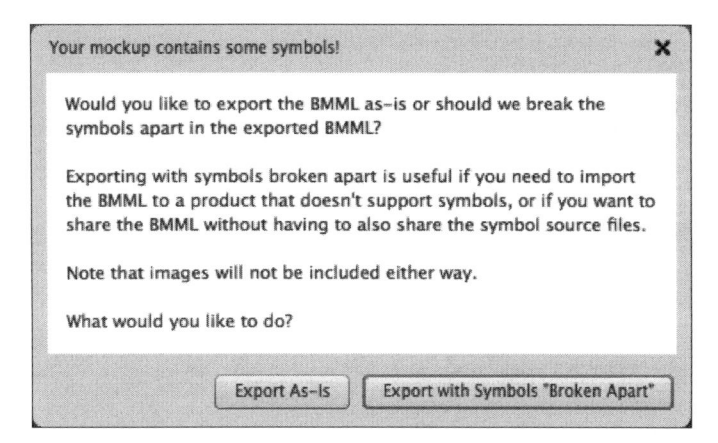

I am sure you will find these dialogue box messages easy to follow. As for the XML, I leave it to you to explore the code itself. You can also visit http://www.balsamiq.com and look through their extensive and very helpful community threads to see what others are saying and doing with XML.

Importing XML

Once copied to the clipboard, XML in its raw form can be pasted by pressing *Control + V/Ctrl + V*, into an email, text file, or any application that accepts code or text. If you paste it back into Balsamiq, the code is transformed back into a wireframe or widget.

Presenting Your Work

You can also import XML using **File | Import Mockup XML**. When you use this tool you will get a popup dialogue box with a text field to import the raw code. Just paste the code from the clipboard into the textbox, as shown in the following screenshot:

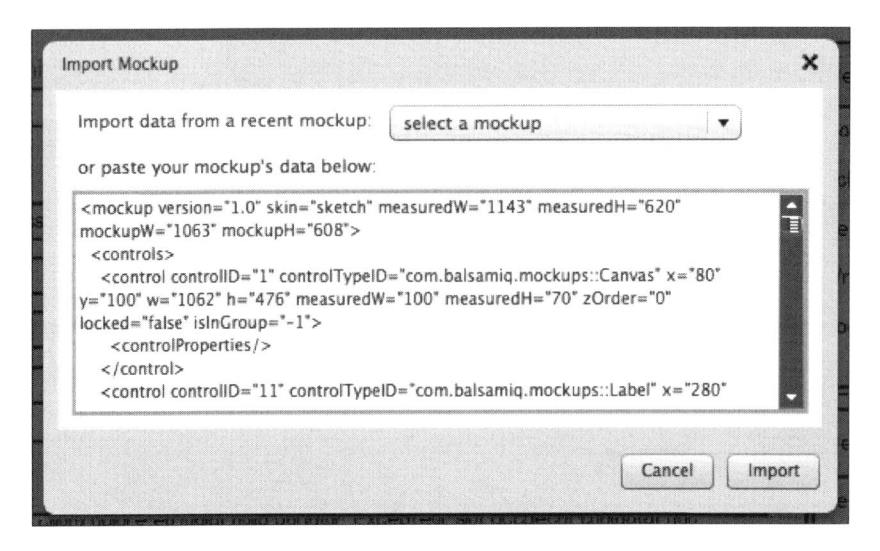

Click on **Import** and the XML code turns back into its original page or wireframe form.

You can also import XML code from another page using the **select a mockup** menu above the textbox. Just select a page from the drop-down menu and its XML code will appear in the textbox.

> Using the **Import Mockup** dialogue box to import XML will overwrite/replace whatever was on the page you are importing to. To avoid losing your work use **Import Mockup XML** only when importing to a blank canvas.

To import XML safely onto an existing page, paste it from the clipboard using **Edit | Paste** or by pressing *Command + V/Ctrl + V*.

Summary

Once again we have covered a lot of material, and you are now left with even more to explore and discover on your own. By now you should have a wireframe and a prototype that incorporate some very cool interactivity, as well as a solid understanding of the tools and widgets that Balsamiq provides. Your next step is to take what you have learned and start building some wireframes on your own. This may take time, practice, and a desire for continued learning, but as you have seen, Balsamiq is easy to learn and fun to use.

In the next and final chapter, I have provided some valuable resources that will help you get to that next level. I am sure you will find them to be educational and motivational as well.

Thanks for joining me on this adventure known as the Balsamiq Wireframes Quickstart Guide. It's been a lot of fun. I hope you agree.

Good luck!

7
Parting Thoughts: Resources and Recommendations

You've made it! Congratulations! Your hard work and dedication has paid off! You are now an expert Balsamiq user! Not feeling like an expert just yet? No worries. Just go back through the chapters and try all the exercises again. Feeling pretty confident? Great! It's time to take your skills to the next level.

To help you with that, I have provided some great resources for developing your creative skills and your creative thinking, not only as a wireframe designer, but also as a designer of the user experience. Remember, it's not just great visual design that makes an interface or product successful. Great design is also determined by how easy it is to navigate and how quickly and clearly the information presented can be understood and acted upon.

With the material covered in this book, you are well on your way to understanding these key concepts. By utilizing the following resources, you will be taking that knowledge to the next level, enabling you to provide not only your best solutions, but more importantly the right ones as well.

The following list shows what we will cover in this chapter:

- More about Balsamiq
- Third party extensions
- More about prototyping
- User experience design

[All the links provided in this chapter can be found at my website: http://www.scottfaranello.com/experience/balsamiq-chapter-links]

More about Balsamiq

Who would better know about Balsamiq than the folks who created it, right? The Balsamiq website is a one-stop shop for all things Balsamiq, including a blog and community support system where real people actually respond!

Love Balsamiq? Hate Balsamiq? Want to see some improvements or perhaps a new feature? Let the folks at Balsamiq know about it. They are very responsive to requests and are most likely already working on it.

Balsamiq blog

The Balsamiq blog is chock-full of posts by Balsamiq's own developers, `http://www.balsamiq.com/blogs`, as shown in the following screenshot:

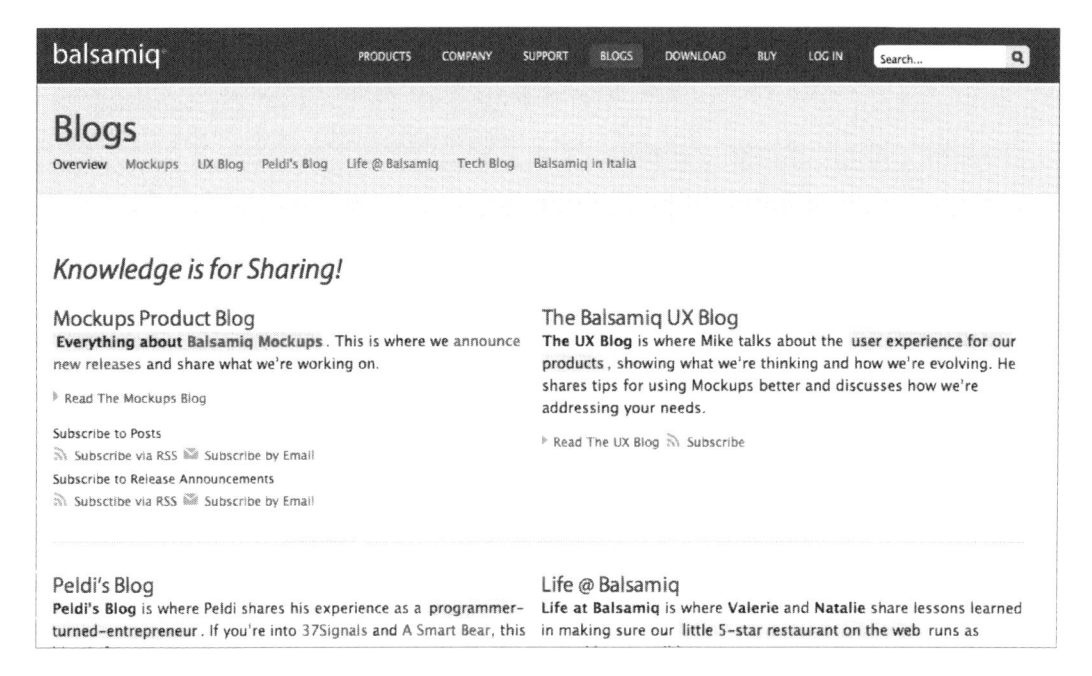

Here, you will find posts on new releases, user experience issues, technical talk and more! You can also subscribe to their posts and follow them on Twitter, and so on. Overall, a great resource that I am sure you will use often. I certainly do.

Chapter 7

Balsamiq support

While Balsamiq is easy to learn, you may still get stumped from time to time and need answers quickly. If so, be sure to check out Balsamiq's support pages at `http://support.balsamiq.com/`, as shown in the following screenshot:

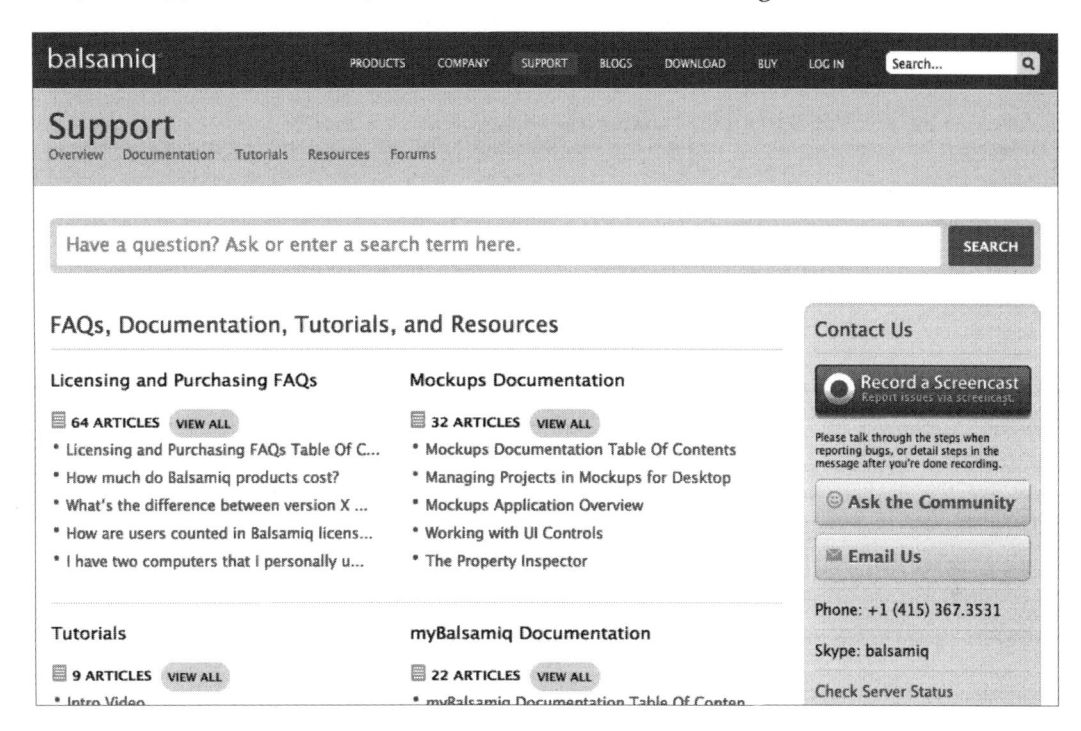

As you can see, support offers articles, FAQs, documentation, tutorials and perhaps my favorite feature on the page…

Record a Screencast

Record a Screencast allows you to record both video and audio while addressing any issue you might be having within the application, as shown in the following screenshot:

Parting Thoughts: Resources and Recommendations

Perform the following steps:

1. Click on the **Record a Screenshot** button to launch the screencast Java app.

    It may take a few seconds or moments to load, depending on your machine and Internet speed.

    > If you don't have Java installed, you may be prompted to install it. If your browser prompts you to do so, click on **Yes**.

2. A screen capture frame will appear to hover on screen, complete with easy-to-follow directions.

3. Navigate to the page you want to share with the support team and click on the record button, as shown in the following screenshot:

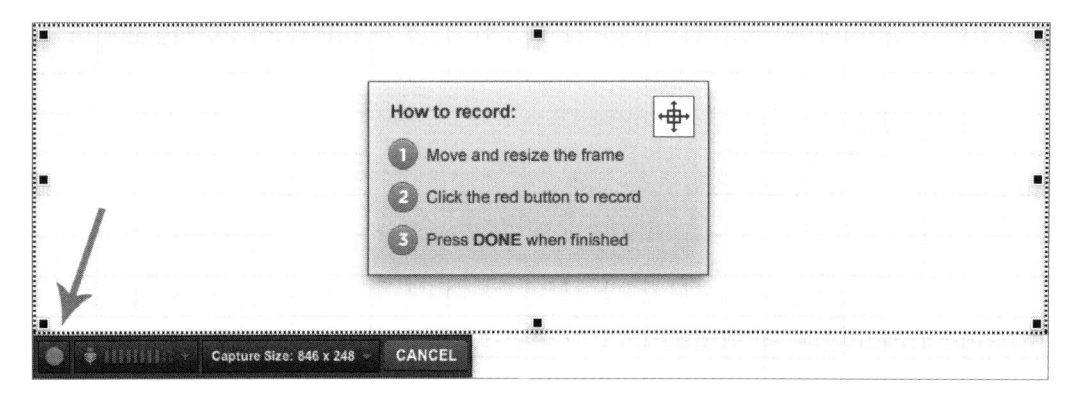

    Wait for the countdown and remember to speak clearly and directly into the microphone if you plan to record your voice, along with your actions on screen.

4. When finished, click on **DONE**, as shown in the following screenshot:

5. View your captured video, fill out the form and upload it to the Balsamiq support team, as shown in the following screenshot:

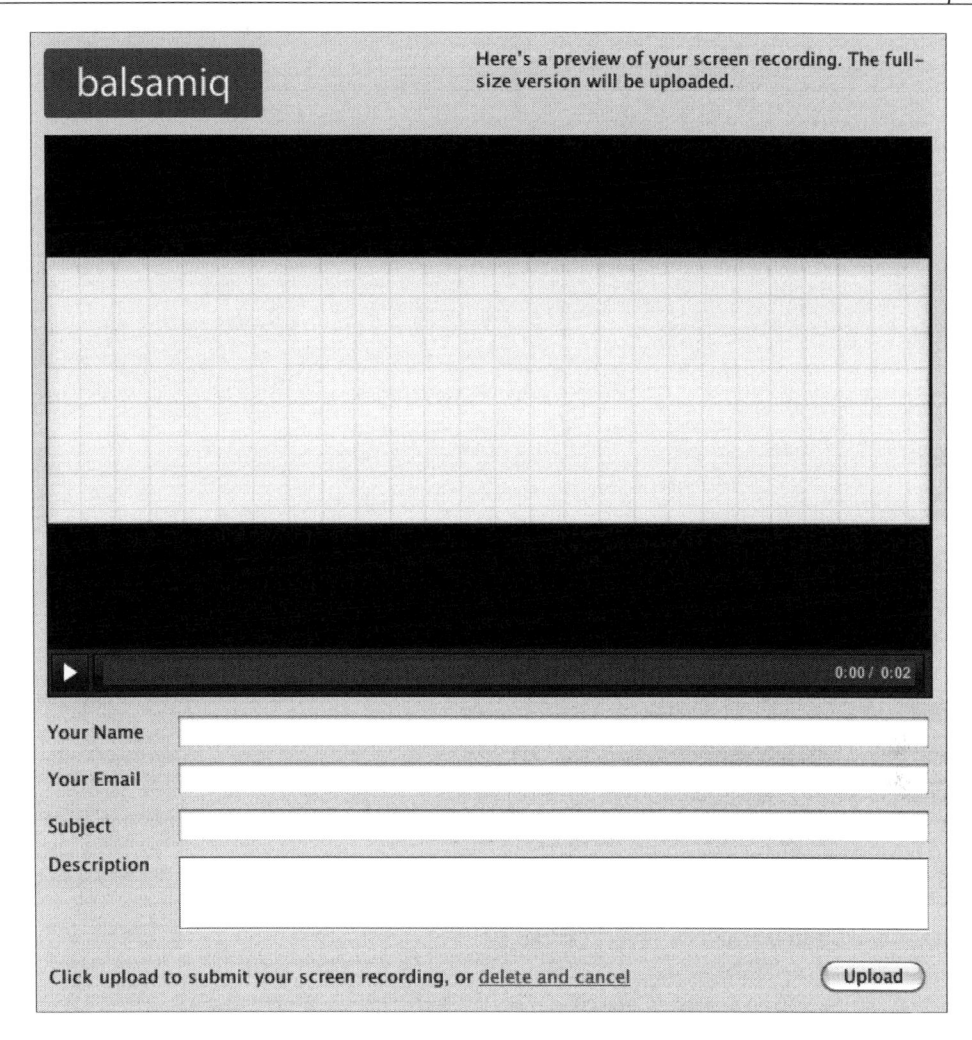

6. Click on **Upload** to submit your recording to the Balsamiq support team.

Ask the community

The other way to make contact is by clicking on the **Ask the Community** button, located just under the screencast button, as shown in the following screenshot:

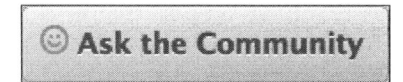

Parting Thoughts: Resources and Recommendations

Ask the Community is an online community of Balsamiq users talking about, what else, Balsamiq, as shown in the following screenshot:

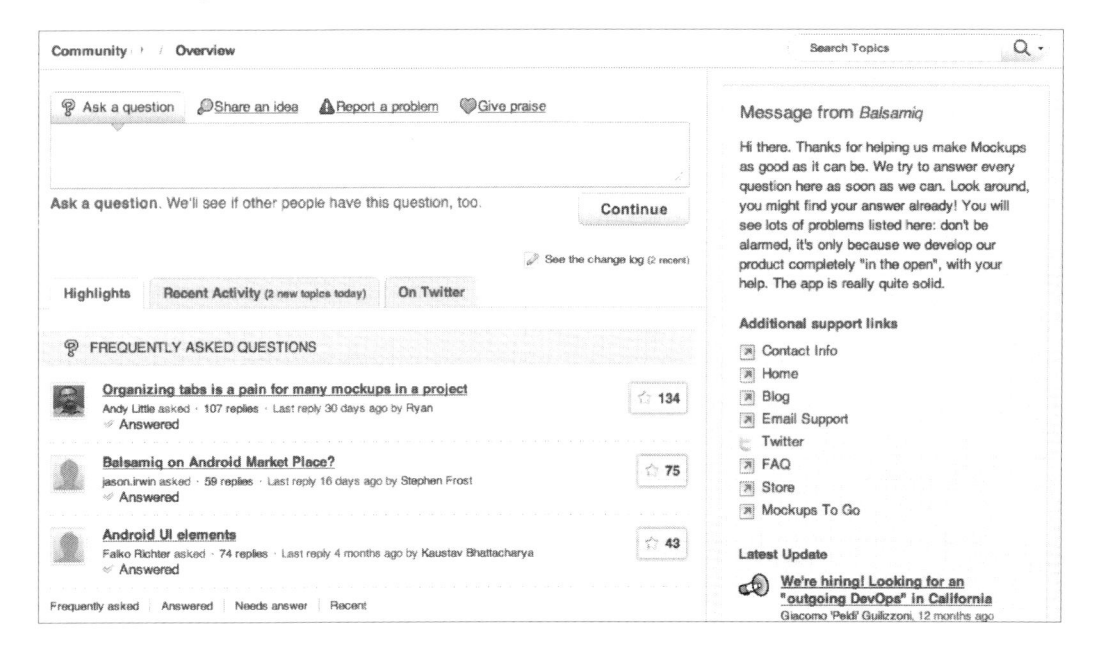

As you can see, there are a number of things you can do here. It's all pretty easy to navigate so I will leave it to you to explore, but explore you must.

To start a new topic of conversation, click on the arrow to the right of the **Community** breadcrumb and select **Topics** in the drop-down menu that appears, as shown in the following screenshot:

Once there, click on the button **Create a new topic**, as shown in the following screenshot:

After that, the rest is up to you. Start a conversation, ask a question, share a tip, tell everyone about this book (had to sneak that one in there), post links to interesting articles about wireframing, whatever! Just try it. You'll like it.

Keyboard shortcuts

I am going to defer to the folks at Balsamiq here, as they provide a very thorough and printable list of keyboard shortcuts. Sorry for the long URL, but I am sure you will find it worth your typing time:

`http://www.balsamiq.com/files/community/balsamiq-keyboard-shortcuts.pdf`.

> As a reminder, all the links in this chapter can be found on my website `http://www.scottfaranello.com/experience/balsamiq-chapter-links/`

Third-party extensions

In addition to the Balsamiq team working hard to bring you a great application, there are also some third-party applications that extend Balsamiq's capabilities even further.

Napkee

If you recall from the previous chapter, Napkee interprets Balsamiq's XML code and produces some very interesting results. In addition to its capability with XML, Napkee can also export files as HTML, CSS, JavaScript and even as Flex Builder 3, all of which can be edited further via a code editor and presented in a web browser.

Just visit `http://www.napkee.com` to get started. While you're there, download a 15-day free trial of the application and be sure to watch the overview video. See what Napkee can do for you.

MockupsToGo

If you recall, we used MockupsToGo, `https://mockupstogo.mybalsamiq.com/projects`, in *Chapter 3*, *Working with Symbols*, to build the blog wireframe, `project_mockup_3.bmml`. As you may recall, MockupsToGo offers Balsamiq widget libraries, which are free to use. All they ask, should you decide to use their handiwork in a publication, is to give them a little credit.

As you will see, MockupsToGo offers all kinds of widget libraries for Android devices, iPhones, social networking, icons for Facebook, Discus, Google Plus, Twitter, web browser layouts, 960 grid systems, Mac OS X desktop controls, Microsoft application widgets, and much, much more. If you want to build it, chances are someone else already has and they are willing to share. Why reinvent the wheel? Browse the categories at MockupsToGo, download the free `.bmml` files and use those hours saved to create some great wireframes.

Reality Mechanic

Designing a mobile app in Balsamiq? Reality Mechanic's Mockups2Android application may just be what you need. Mockups2Android, `http://www.realitymechanic.com`, provides the ability to upload Balsamiq files directly to your Android phone for real-world click throughs, user testing, prototyping and stakeholder reviews. Now that's cool!

Be sure to check out their video tutorials as well, to understand how it all works.

LiveMockups

Similar to Mockups2Android, LiveMockups provides similar viewing functionality for the iPhone and iPad.

Visit `http://livemockups.openium.fr` to learn more.

Wirify by Volkside

Wirify, `http://www.wirify.com`, is a free app that turns any web page into a Balsamiq-like wireframe in an instant. Simply drag the Wirify bookmarklet into your browser's bookmark toolbar, find a site whose layout you want to wirify, click the bookmark, and voilà! Instant wireframe!

Of course, if you want to edit what you just created, you will have to pay for it. But then again, you could just recreate what you see on the screen directly into Balsamiq and it won't cost you anything. If nothing else, Wirify is a great tool to see how some of your favorite websites might look as wireframes. It is also a good source of inspiration in terms of layout, spatial relationships of shapes, placement of elements, and so on. Give it a try.

Project management

As you have seen, Balsamiq makes sharing and exporting files easy. But, there are times when sharing files across large projects with multiple team members requires more careful tracking and greater organization than simply e-mailing files to one another. In situations like this, large projects are best served by using project management tools like Google Drive, Confluence, Jira, and Wiki. Balsamiq offers a variety of easy-to-install plugins that interact seamlessly with these tools, making file sharing across large projects very easy.

To learn more about these plugins and the project management tools they support, visit `http://balsamiq.com/products/mockups/plugins`.

Further reading

Balsamiq is a great tool, but it is just that. Learning about customer experience, user experience and interface design takes time, dedication, great interest, and a passion for delivering simple yet intuitive designs that people respond to. You need not only know what you are doing, but also be able to answer why you are doing it.

To that point, I now want to share with you some great resources, both in print and online, that will help you get to that next level.

Books

The list that follows is by no means complete or exhaustive. It is merely a starting point. You will find that each book offers great insight into the world of user experience, design, and the psychology around it. As you will see, there are quite a few to choose from. Pick one and start reading. When you are finished, pick another and read that one too. There is no hurry. Just enjoy the process. I do have to warn you though, once you start delving deeper into the world of user experience and design, you may not want to stop.

- *The Design of Everyday Things*, Donald Norman, Doubleday Business, 1990
- *User Experience Re-mastered*, Chauncey Wilson, Morgan Kaufmann, 2009
- *Simple and Usable Web, Mobile, and Interaction Design*, Giles Colborne, New Riders Press, 2010
- *A Project Guide to UX Design: For user experience designers in the field or in the making*, Russ Unger and Carolyn Chandler, New Riders Press, 2009

Parting Thoughts: Resources and Recommendations

- *The User Is Always Right: A Practical Guide to Creating and Using Personas for the Web*, Steve Mulder and Ziv Yaar, New Riders Press, 2006
- *Prioritizing Web Usability*, Jakob Nielson and Hoa Loranger, New Riders Press, 2006
- *Mental Models: Aligning Design Strategy with Human Behavior*, Indi Young, Rosenfeld Media, 2008
- *Don't Make Me Think: A Common Sense Approach to Web Usability, 2nd Edition*, Steve Krug, New Riders Press, 2005
- *Communicating Design: Developing Web Site Documentation for Design and Planning, 2nd Edition*, Dan Brown, New Riders Press, 2010
- *Designing with the Mind in Mind: Simple Guide to Understanding User Interface Design Rules*, Jeff Johnson, Morgan Kaufmann, 2010
- *The Usability Engineering Lifecycle: A Practitioner's Handbook for User Interface Design*, Deborah J. Mayhew, Morgan Kaufmann, 1999
- *The Inmates Are Running the Asylum: Why High Tech Products Drive Us Crazy and How To Restore The Sanity*, Alan Cooper, Sams, 1999

> For an even longer list of titles, stop by my site at http://www.scottfaranello.com/experience/balsamiq-book-list/
> Prepare to be overwhelmed at the sheer volume of information on the subject.

Usability websites

The following websites also provide a mountain of information about user experience design and related topics. The sites I have listed are some of my favorites and ones where you will find more information than you can possibly process in one sitting. But then, that's what bookmarks are for.

The following is a list of URLs with descriptions that are taken verbatim from their respective sites:

- `http://www.alistapart.com/`: A List Apart explores the design, development, and meaning of web content, with a special focus on web standards and best practices.
- `http://www.uxbooth.com/`: A publication by, and for, the User Experience Community.

Chapter 7

- `http://boxesandarrows.com/`: Journal dedicated to discussing, improving and promoting the work of the information architecture community.
- `http://www.smashingmagazine.com/`: An online magazine for professional Web designers and developers, with a focus on useful techniques and best practices.
- `http://www.useit.com/`: Research findings from many usability studies 1994-2012. Web design guidelines. Usability training courses.
- `http://www.humanfactors.com/home/usability.asp`: Human Factors International (HFI) is the world's largest company specializing in user-centered design.
- `http://www.uxforthemasses.com/`: Articles about encouraging people, be they developers, designers, students, product managers or even just interested bystanders to take a dip into the stimulating, refreshing and thirst-quenching world of user experience (UX).
- `http://uxmag.com/`: Created to be a central, one-stop resource for everything related to user experience.
- `http://www.usercentric.com/`: A global user experience research firm.
- `http://webusability-blog.com/`: A team of Belgium based usability experts and information architects.

One final tip

If you are a professional Usability Expert, User Experience Designer, Wireframe Architect, or someone who aspires to be, then LinkedIn is for you, `http://www.linkedin.com`.

This is a site I use often and it has helped me in my work and career tremendously. One area of the site I find very useful is the Groups and Associations section. This is a place where you can join various groups of like-minded folks who are sharing information and communicating on a large scale.

For example, check out UX Professionals, Usability Practitioners, UsabilityMatters.Org, User Experience Group, User Experience Recruiting, and others. These groups, and many others like it, are a great resource for asking questions, getting answers, sharing tips and tricks, and a great place overall to share knowledge and to feel like part of a community.

You really can't go wrong. Give it a try!

Summary

Well, there you have it; my brief, but very valuable list of great resources to fuel your knowledge, creativity and inspiration. Even though our journey ends here, it is really just the beginning for you. What you have gained by learning Balsamiq is a great first step in your future of building intuitive, well-designed interfaces. If you are already working in the field and chose this book to learn more about Balsamiq and how to prepare and present your work, then you now have a great new tool at your disposal. Either way, be sure to keep this book handy for reference whenever you need it.

It's been a pleasure being your guide. I hope you have enjoyed it as much as I have. Until next time, keep wireframing, designing, learning, and pushing your creativity to new heights and new directions. You will be better off for it and more importantly, so will your end users.

Good luck and have fun!

Index

A

additional interactivity
  adding 94
  interactive checkbox 95-97
  popup form, adding 100
  text row, adding 97-99
additional tips
  Auto-Size 88
  Lorem ipsum 87
  Sketch it! 87
Adobe Air 9
align tool 33, 34
A List Apart
  URL 120
Application Bar, Balsamiq application window
  about 15
  Full Screen (Presentation Mode) 16
  Quick Add tool 15, 16
  Show Markup 16
  Tool Bar 16
Application menu, Balsamiq
  about 10, 11
  Close All 11
  Export All Mockups to PDF 13
  Export All Mockups to PNG 13
  Export Image to Clipboard 13
  Export Mockup XML 13
  Export to PNG Image 12
  Import Mockup XML 14
  New Clone of Current Mockup 11
  Save All 11
application window, Balsamiq
  about 14
  Application Bar 15

  canvas 18
  File Browser 18
  UI Library 17
Ask the Community button 115
Auto-Size 88

B

Balsamiq
  about 8, 119
  additional interactivity 94
  additional tips 86
  application 10
  Application menu 10
  application view 14
  books 119
  data, deciphering 55
  data, formatting 55
  data tables 53
  data table tips 59
  exporting functionality 102
  features 8
  formatting tools 82
  Icon Library 74-77
  icons, exploring 71-73
  icons, importing 73, 74
  images 77
  installing 8
  keyboard shortcuts 117
  Markup widgets 101
  pages, linking 91, 92
  Property Inspector 20
  prototyping 89
  symbols 37
  text, working with 82
  third party extensions 117

tip 121
trial, versus paid version 10
usability websites 120
XML 106
files, organizing 22
project, building 21
project files 21
Balsamiq blog
  about 112
  URL 112
Balsamiq files
  naming 22
  naming, alphabetically 22
  numbering 22
  organizing 22
Balsamiq installation
  about 8, 9
  system requisites 8
Balsamiq Mockups
  versus, myBalsamiq 10
Balsamiq Prototyping 7
Balsamiq support
  about 113
  Ask the Community button 115
  Create a new topic button 116
  Record a Screenshot button 113, 114
  URL 113
Bring Forward tool 28
Bring to Front tool 28

C

canvas, Balsamiq application window 18
close all, file menu 11

D

data
  columns, creating 56
  columns, removing 56
  deciphering 55
  formatting 55
  grid form elements 56, 57
  text alignment, controlling 57, 58
  width, controlling 57, 58

data table
  data, keeping manageable 67
  data, keeping readable 67
  fornatting 67
  in wireframe project 60, 61
  Mac and PC compatibility issues 68, 69
  maximum column width 68
  table columns, padding 68
  text, aligning 68
data tables
  building 53, 54
data table tips
  about 59
  scroll bar, adding 60
  table row, highlighting 59

E

Export All Mockups to PDF, file menu 13
Export All Mockups to PNG, file menu 13
exporting functionality
  about 102
  using 107
Export Mockup XML, file menu 13
Export to PNG Image, file menu 12

F

File Browser, Balsamiq application window
  about 18
  options 18, 19
Full Screen (Presentation Mode) 16

I

Icon Library 74-77
icons
  exploring 71-73
  importing 73, 74
images
  about 77
  copying, to project assets 79, 80
  cropping 80, 81
  Image not found 80
  Load Image window 78
image widgets 32

Import Mockup XML, file menu 14
installation
  Balsamiq 8

K

keyboard shortcuts
  about 117
  URL 117

L

layering 26, 28
layers
  rearranging 27
linked pages
  presentation mode 92
link types, presentation mode
  invisible links 92
  visible links 93
LiveMockups
  about 118
  URL 118
Lorem ipsum
  about 87
  URL 87

M

Mac and PC compatibility issues, data table 68
markup
  about 101
  adding, to wireframe 101
Markup widgets 101
master page 40
Mockups2Android application 118
MockupsToGo
  about 117
  URL 117

N

Napkee
  about 117
  URL 107, 117
New Clone of Current Mockup, file menu 11

P

pages
  linking 91, 92
presentation mode, linked pages
  Edit this mockup 94
  link types 92
  Show Markup 94
  toggling 93
project
  align tool 33
  body copy 34
  building 23
  design and layout 29
  images, adding 32
  implementing 29
  layering 26-28
  layers, grouping 28
  Rectangle/Canvas/Panel 30, 31
  text, adding 31, 32
  UI Library 24
  Video Player widget, adding 25
  Video Player widget, positioning 25, 26
  widget, adding 24
project files
  about 21
  downloading 21
project management tools 119
Property Inspector 20
prototyping
  about 89
  symbols, revisiting 90

R

Reality Mechanic
  about 118
  URL 118
Record a Screenshot button 113, 114
Rectangle/Canvas/Panel 30

S

save all, file menu 11
saved symbols
  locating 39
Send Backward tool 28
Send to Back tool 28

[125]

Sketch it! 87
symbol library
  creating 47, 48
symbols
  about 37
  adding, to multiple pages 44
  adding, to project 48, 49
  as master page 40
  copying 45
  creating 38, 39, 46
  deleting 43
  deleting, all pages 43
  deleting, page by page 43
  double-clicking 46
  dragging 46
  footer, adding to pages 47
  header symbol, adding to wireframe project 44
  modifying 40
  pasting 45
  sharing 50
  sharing, across multiple projects 50, 51
  sharing, project by project 50
  text, adding 46, 47
Symbols.bmml 40
symbols, modifying
  about 40
  additional ways 42
  all pages 41
  Break Apart button 42
  Edit Source button 42
  page-by-page basis 40
  Project Assets section 42
  reverting to saved feature 42

T

text
  formatting styles, combining 84
  single line text, versus paragraph 84, 85
text formatting 82, 83
text tools 83
third party extensions
  about 117
  LiveMockups 118
  MockupsToGo 117

Napkee 117
project management tools 119
Reality Mechanic 118
Wirify 118

U

UI Library, Balsamiq application window
  about 17
  using 17
usability websites 120, 121
User Experience Community
  URL 120

W

wireframe project
  symbols, adding 44
wireframe project, revising
  action bar 61-63
  data table 63-65
  paging 65, 66
wireframes
  entire project, exporting to PNG 105
  exporting, to PDF 102, 103
  exporting, to PNG 104
  image, exporting to clipboard 105
  individual elements, exporting to PNG 104
  single page, exporting to PNG 104
Wirify
  about 118
  URL 118

X

XML
  about 106
  exporting 106
  importing 107, 108

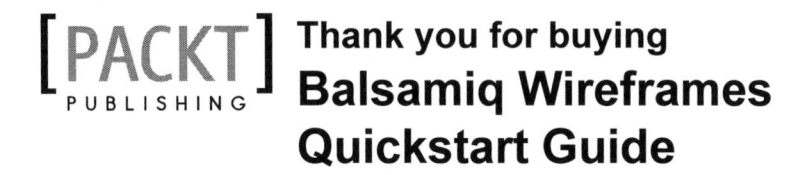

[PACKT PUBLISHING] Thank you for buying Balsamiq Wireframes Quickstart Guide

About Packt Publishing

Packt, pronounced 'packed', published its first book "*Mastering phpMyAdmin for Effective MySQL Management*" in April 2004 and subsequently continued to specialize in publishing highly focused books on specific technologies and solutions.

Our books and publications share the experiences of your fellow IT professionals in adapting and customizing today's systems, applications, and frameworks. Our solution based books give you the knowledge and power to customize the software and technologies you're using to get the job done. Packt books are more specific and less general than the IT books you have seen in the past. Our unique business model allows us to bring you more focused information, giving you more of what you need to know, and less of what you don't.

Packt is a modern, yet unique publishing company, which focuses on producing quality, cutting-edge books for communities of developers, administrators, and newbies alike. For more information, please visit our website: www.packtpub.com.

Writing for Packt

We welcome all inquiries from people who are interested in authoring. Book proposals should be sent to author@packtpub.com. If your book idea is still at an early stage and you would like to discuss it first before writing a formal book proposal, contact us; one of our commissioning editors will get in touch with you.

We're not just looking for published authors; if you have strong technical skills but no writing experience, our experienced editors can help you develop a writing career, or simply get some additional reward for your expertise.

Axure RP 6 Prototyping Essentials

ISBN: 978-1-84969-164-2　　　Paperback: 446 pages

Creating highly compelling, interactive prototypes with Axure that will impress and excite decision makers

1. Quickly simulate complex interactions for a wide range of applications without any programming knowledge

2. Acquire timesaving methods for constructing and annotating wireframes, interactive prototypes, and UX specifications

3. A hands-on guide that walks you through the iterative process of UX prototyping with Axure

Mastering Adobe Captivate 6

ISBN: 978-1-84969-244-1　　　Paperback: 476 pages

Create professional SCORM-compliant eLearning content with Adode Captivate

1. Step by step tutorial to build three projects including a demonstration, a simulation and a random SCORM-compliant quiz featuring all possible question slides.

2. Enhance your projects by adding interactivity, animations, sound and more

3. Publish your project in a wide variety of formats enabling virtually any desktop and mobile devices to play your e-learning content

4. Deploy your e-Learning content on a SCORM or AICC-compliant LMS

Please check **www.PacktPub.com** for information on our titles

[PACKT] PUBLISHING

Dreamweaver CS5.5 Mobile and Web Development with HTML5, CSS3, and jQuery

ISBN: 978-1-84969-158-1 Paperback: 284 pages

Harness the cutting edge features of Dreamweaver for mobile and web development

1. Create web pages in Dreamweaver using the latest technology and approach
2. Add multimedia and interactivity to your websites
3. Optimize your websites for a wide range of platforms and build mobile apps with Dreamweaver

OmniGraffle 5 Diagramming Essentials

ISBN: 978-1-84969-076-8 Paperback: 380 pages

Create better diagrams with less effort using OmniGraffle

1. Produce high-quality professional-looking diagrams that communicate information much better than words
2. Makes diagramming fun and simple for Macintosh users
3. Master the art of illustrating your ideas with OmniGraffle
4. Learn to draw engaging charts and graphs to grasp your viewers' attention to your presentations

Please check **www.PacktPub.com** for information on our titles

13230085R00080

Printed in Great Britain
by Amazon.co.uk, Ltd.,
Marston Gate.